D1825199

Chakra Meditation

21 Days Guided Meditation to Awaken your Spiritual Power, Reduce Stress & Anxiety and Improve Awareness of Psychic Abilities with Reiki Healing Exercises

By

New Mindfulness Lab

physical, digital and audio unless express consent of the Publisher is provided beforehand. Any additional rights reserved.

Furthermore, the information that can be found within the pages described forthwith shall be considered both accurate and truthful when it comes to the recounting of facts. As such, any use, correct or incorrect, of the provided information will render the Publisher free of responsibility as to the actions taken outside of their direct purview. Regardless, there are zero scenarios where the original author or the Publisher can be deemed liable in any fashion for any damages or hardships that may result from any of the information discussed herein.

Additionally, the information in the following pages is intended only for informational purposes and should thus be thought of as universal. As befitting its nature, it is presented without assurance regarding its prolonged validity or interim quality. Trademarks that are mentioned are done without written consent and can in no way be considered an endorsement from the trademark holder.

Table of Contents

Introduction

Congratulations on downloading your copy of *Chakra Meditation: 21 Days Guided Meditation to Awaken your Spiritual Power, Reduce Stress & Anxiety and Improve Awareness of Psychic Abilities with Reiki Healing Exercises.* My hope is that it includes everything that you are searching for on the subject of meditation, stress reduction and building your psychic abiltities as well as helpful information which you can start to apply to your life today to bring you a deep appreciation with your natural born gifts and how to use them.

In this comprehensive guide, you will out the history and basics or meditation, Reiki and several psychic abilities that we can all tap into. There is a wide range of exercises that you can perform to strengthen your intuition, your psychic abilities as well as meditation techniques to apply to your 21 day meditation which focuses on each chakra for three days.

The book goes further to give you guidance and clarity on the purpose and responsibilities of each chakra as well as which body parts that they are associated with. This will give you a better understanding about what chakra may be blocked if you having issues with the associated body parts. Knowing where the problems lie will help you to know what direction to go after the initial 21 day chakra meditation is complete.

You will also find out more of what symptoms are experienced on a physical and emotional level with each chakra and general advice in how to balance your chakras once again. You will then have a guided meditation for the duration of three days per chakra. Following the meditations and exercises are going to help each of your chakras to become balanced and energized.

There is also a chapter dedicated to how to keep your energy levels up during the day. Using protective and counter intuitive approaches, you will be able to keep others from taking your energy as well as it bleeding out of your system.

Once you have completed the book, you have knowledge in how to start healing your body from the inside out using the meditation techniques and exercises. There are plenty of books on Chakra Meditation, and thanks again for choosing this one! Every effort was made to ensure that it is full of as much useful information as possible.

Chapter 1: Introduction to Meditation

Meditation has become more popular around the turn of the millennium, but it goes back thousands of years. The word *meditation* comes from the Latin word *meditatum* which means *to ponder*. It has been practiced in different forms throughout many different locations and traditions, but it originated in India between 5,000 and 3,500 BCE from evidence of temple and cave carvings. It was practiced first by the Vedic sages and cave yogis, with the first written evidence in the Vedas, a Hindu spiritual scripture, in 1,500 BCE after being passed down orally for centuries.

A Timeline of Meditation Development & History

The sages and yogis were the religious people who wandered around the Indian subcontinent as ascetics. Through the meditative practices, they were able to connect with universal forces and transcendental reality known as the creator of Brahman in the Vedic scriptures. From these texts, there have been hundreds of techniques and lineages of this information being shared through the generations.

It is thought that the original technique was through gazing or mantra meditation. Gazing is where a specific object is looked upon with intent whereas mantra meditation consists of a phrase of Sanskrit words which would create a specific sound and vibration depending on the purpose of the mantra. The modern movement of Yoga has basis in meditation along with breathing exercises coupled with postures and also originated in India.

Meditation continued to be practiced in the branch of Hinduism known as Buddhism. In the 6th century BCE, the prince known as Siddhartha Gautama renounced his royal life to live a life of an ascetic so that he could gain enlightenment. Through his journey, he learned philosophy and meditation techniques through the rishis, or sages. Throughout this process, he diverted from the Hindu traditions and created what is known as Buddhism today. He was successful in his goal of attaining enlightenment and became the Buddha. He then dedicated his life to teaching spiritual awakening and meditation. Over the course of decades, he was able to teach thousands of people.

In modern times, there are several lineages which have their own styles of meditation known as Walking Meditation, Loving-Kindness, Samatha and Vipassana. These types of meditations spread to the West over the centuries, and are the most widely practiced forms of meditation today.

During the same time period of Buddha, there were three religions which were created that had their own teachings on meditation. These were Confucianism, Taoism and Jainism.

Confucianism centers around morality and community. Their form of meditation has a focus on self-improvement and self-contemplation, and is name Jing Zuo. Confucianism is still popular today, but is mainly found in Asia.

Taoism is focused on creating a union with the Tao, or cosmic nature and life. Their meditation technique helps with the generation, transformation and circulation of the energy within the body, known to them as Chi. This type of meditation aids in finding inner peace by unifying with the body, spirit and Tao and quietens the mind and body.

Jainism's meditation technique uses self-inquiry, visualizations, breath awareness, gazing and mantra repetition. Their religion is based on the ascetic lifestyle and focuses on non-violence, contemplation, self-discipline and self-purification.

The Greek philosophers of Aristotle and Plato developed their own technique of meditation through the influence of the yogis and sages of India. This happened during the time of Alexander the Great's military efforts in India between 327 – 325 BCE). Meditation was not the only influence to the Greek philosopher's system as they admired the sages' immunity to discomfort and pain and their particular disinterest in pleasure and their fearlessness of death.

The meditation technique that was created by the Greek philosophers was known as navel-gazing. This involves deep contemplation of a single issue of oneself. In later years, the philosophers Plotinus and Philo of Alexandria also created a type of meditation that focused on concentration. However, once Christianity started to dominate Europe, the influence of Eastern thought was abruptly cut. However, the ideas started to resurface during the 20th century when Europe and the East started to communicate once again.

The Christians started their own type of meditation which also involved repetition of a religious phrase or word, much like a mantra, and they also would sit in silent contemplation upon God. One method of meditation practiced by the Hesychasm Christians was known as the Jesus Prayer which was developed in Greece between the 10th and 14th centuries. It is believed that this tradition of Christians were in contact with the sufis and Indian sages which influenced their type of meditation.

During the 8th century, a school of Buddhism known as Zen was founded by an Indian-Persian monk by the name of Bodhidharma. He had traveled to China to teach meditation in which the lineage of Chan was born which was adapted by Vietnam, Japan and Korea. All of these versions of meditation were known as Zen which had a massive influence on the Chinese culture and Taoism. Because of the influence from a collective of countries and traditions, Zen meditation is quite unique.

The meditation technique is known as Zazen and is still a popular method of meditation in the West today. Some lineages of Zen also have a method of meditation by the name of Koans. In this type of meditation, the teachers as their students to ponder on a puzzle or riddle in the form of phrases, questions and stories to discover the greater truths about themselves and the world.

The tradition of the Islam Sufis date back as far as 1,400 years, and they were influenced as well by Indian traditions. Their forms of meditation include gazing, the use of mantras and focused breathing exercises. Their practices are designed to solidify their connection with Allah, or God, and also include a method in which they will whirl around in circles to create this effect. In fact, this whirling method is still used in Turkey today.

The esoteric Jewish tradition of the Kabbalah had also developed their own forms of meditation during the 11th century. Their methods include deep contemplation of prayers, symbols, names of God and philosophical principles. They also would reflect upon the principle of the Tree of Life which is a representation of individual beauty, uniqueness and personal development. Similar to a tree, the branches growing up to the sky is a symbol of an individual becoming stronger as they strive for new experiences, wisdom and greater knowledge.

During the 16ᵗʰ century, the Eastern traditions were beginning to be translated into Western languages. The scriptures that were translated were the Buddhist Sutras, the Bhagavad Gita and the Upanishads. Two centuries later, Buddhist was a study for the intellectuals in the West with the philosopher Schopenhauer being one of the biggest admirers of the Eastern traditions and teachings. With the Transcendentalist movement in the United States, Henry David Thoreau and Ralph Waldo Emerson had deep ties to Eastern spirituality and philosophy.

During the 20ᵗʰ century, Swami Vivekananda had come to the United States to introduce meditation and yoga teachings. His debut of his philosophy was presented at the Parliament of Religions which took place in Chicago in 1893. This sparked great interest in the practice of meditation and was supported by the Transcendentalist movement as well. As a result, many well-known Indian babas, or teachers, moved to the United States like Swami Rama, Maharishi Mahesh Yogi and Paramahansa Yogananda to teach their methods of meditation. The Buddhists teachers also made their way to the United States teaching Tibetan, Theravada and Zen meditation.

Due to the influx and availability of Eastern teachings, the masters were able to create a large following which laid the groundwork to the ancient traditions to be taught and practiced today. This movement was furthered due to scientific studies being released that showed that mediation practices benefited those who were not specifically seeking spiritual enlightenment. For those who were not wanting to meditate for spiritual reasons, the teachings had to be modified to remove the spiritual context. Also, the practices were adapted for the Western way of life to be more simple as most of the western disciples would not be able to follow the strict guidelines which are found in the East.

During the 20th century, scientific studies on meditation started to emerge. The first tests were conducted in 1936 and the first collection of these studies were published in 1977 by James Funderburk who was a follower of Swami Rama. In fact, Swami Rama was the first of the Indian yogis who agreed to be studied by Western scientists. These tests were conducted in the 1960s where the yogi performed different practices such as voluntarily controlling his body temperature, blood pressure and heartbeat. Before these tests were conducted, it was believed that these were involuntary actions of the body.

Due to these discoveries, scientists had interests in researching meditation even further.

Over the course of the next five decades, meditation has been extensively researched. With the advances in technology, the scientists were able to dig deeper to discover other benefits that meditation can have for the mind and body. Monks and llamas from the Zen and Tibetan traditions had been also studied which demonstrated the results of mind-over-body practices. During the early years of the 1970s, Dr. Herbert Benson of Harvard University created a major shift in the thought that meditation was solely for religious purposes. Through his research, he was able to show that meditation could be used for healthcare purposes as well.

As a result, meditation during the 21st century has become widely popular and secularized. There are still spiritual meditation practices which are used today in the Western countries, but most use the secular approach to realize the benefits to the overall wellness of the mind and body. The people who meditate regularly report they have positive changes in the mental and physical wellbeing in their lives as well as having a more peaceful and calm outlook.

The Basics of Meditation

There are many different types of meditation, but they are all based upon the same basic principles. Before you start your meditation practices, you need to prepare yourself so that you are able to get the most out of your time.

Preparing for Meditation

Following these basic steps are going to help ease you into your meditation practice.

❖ Find a place which you are going to be comfortable sitting. It does not need to be completely quiet as a small amount of background noise will be fine.

❖ Wear clothing that you feel relaxed and comfortable in. If you are wearing constrictive clothing such as a scarf, belt or tie, you likely will want to loosen these ahead of time. If you are wearing shoes that are tight or heels, you will need to remove them.

❖ Whether you decide to lay down or sit in a chair, you want to have your back straight, your chin tucked in slightly and your neck muscles relaxed. You can place your hands where they feel comfortable on your knees or your lap if you are sitting. When laying down, you can lay your hands next to your body or fold them over your stomach or chest.

❖ Choose a time that you will be able to perform meditation each day by coupling it with a concrete routine such as brushing your teeth. Getting yourself in the habit of spending time in quiet contemplation will create a ripple effect of benefits in your life.

❖ Knowing your purpose and intention of wanting to incorporate a meditation practice in your life will help drive you. If you know what your motivation is to practice, you will be more likely to build your habit of practicing meditation.

❖ There is no such thing as a good or bad meditation. There are going to be some days you will not connect with the passing thoughts in your mind and others where you cannot stop engaging. This is okay. Be kind and remind yourself that this practice is to ultimately teach you patience. Continue the next day with a clean slate and do not stop because you think you are doing it wrong. It simply is not true. Over time you will find that your mind will be less distracted with thoughts and the process will be much simpler.

Basic Meditation Exercises

There are several approaches that one can take when wanting to incorporate a meditation practice. Try the following exercises to see which one works best for you personally.

Mindfulness Meditation Exercise

This type of meditation is going to strengthen your mindfulness and attention. It will help you to stay present in this given moment and anchor yourself in your purpose without judgement in the here and now.

Step 1: Lie or sit down in a comfortable position. This can be on the floor or in a chair. If you are sitting in a chair, be sure to have your feet flat on the ground during meditation. If you choose to sit on the floor, you can make yourself more comfortable with a meditation cushion or yoga mat. You can sit in a cross legged position or sitting on your bent legs. Whatever position you choose, you need to be comfortable during the entire meditation.

Step 2: Close your eyes and breathe naturally.

Step 3: While you are breathing, take notice of the movement of the body with each inhalation and exhalation. Focus on your belly, rib cage, shoulders and chest movements. Continue to breathe naturally during this process. If your mind should wander, bring your focus back on your breathing.

Step 4: Continue this practice between two and three minutes if you have never practiced meditation before. Build up the time each day to a time frame which you are comfortable.

Step 5: Slowly open your eyes and take your time moving.

There is no set time you must meditate, but it is helpful if you are able to quiet your mind for a minimum of 15 minutes each day. You will want to perform your meditation practice at the same time each day. Continuing to focus on your breathing will help to clear your mind. Once you master this technique, you will be able to perform other types of meditation with ease.

Evaluate your Meditation Practice

Especially when you are beginning with your meditation practices, it is important to evaluate when you had learned during the meditation practice. Ask yourself the following questions:

- ❖ How many breaths did it take before your mind wandered away from focusing on your breathing?
- ❖ Did you take note of how much more busy your mind was, even when you were trying to clear your mind?
- ❖ Were you getting caught up in your thoughts when this occurred?

Knowing the answers to these questions will give you deeper insight as to how your mind goes about its daily tasks. It also shows you that the mind can be overworked and full of nonsense that can take you away from focusing on what is important. Know that you are not alone. These thoughts racing through your mind is the product of not being present in the current moment, and we have grown comfortable in allowing our thoughts take over our brains.

Practicing meditation helps to calm down this freight train of thoughts and allows you to recognize these thoughts as passing ideas. Being able to see your thoughts in a different perspective will allow you to not have to become involved in every thought that comes up in your mind. They simply come and go, and the more that you practice meditation, the more the thoughts and mind will calm down.

Remedying Common Mistakes for Meditation Practice

When you are just starting out, there are many obstacles that you can create which will hinder your confidence or progress with your meditation routine. Let us go over several common ways that you are cutting yourself short from your true potential of your meditations and how to remedy or avoid them in the first place.

It is common as a beginner to feel an array of feelings such as resistant, overwhelmed, anxious, fearful, bored, restless or a combination thereof. Once you get over these initial feelings, you will notice them quickly vanish away. Remember, your mind is used to being busy all of the time. You are trying to improve that by slowing down your thought processes, and it is a result that will come with time.

You are able to help these initial thoughts by keeping to your scheduled time for meditation. There should be no excuses, and you always can make the time to sit in silence for 10 or 15 minutes a day. Doing something out of the norm can bring about these feelings, but put them aside just for these few minutes a day, and you will notice that they will not continue to come up before you meditation practice.

If you are not able to practice every single day, do not beat yourself up. Of course you are going to find the benefits of meditation much more quickly practicing each day. However, the most important thing for beginners to realize is that they are taking baby steps in creating a new habit. The time you are able to dedicate to meditation, the more you are going to get out of it, but this does not mean that you must stress yourself out in the process.

Bottom line is, you need to listen to your body. If you are in a state of stress and being overwhelmed, you are very likely going to benefit from taking the time to meditate. Setting a time 2 to 3 times a week even will be more of a benefit if you waited, let us say a month, in between meditation sessions.

Feeling sleepy is another common issue to where you may even be nodding off during your meditation. This is a very common theme for beginners. When your mind is so used to being on the go, it can confuse your stillness with relaxation, causing you to feel more tired. After you continue the meditation practices, you will start to rewire your brain so that it understands you are not resting because you want to sleep.

Three ways that you are able to help this situation is to open a window so that there is a breeze in your meditation room. You can also set your meditation time during the morning or when your mind is more alert. If you are laying down, sit up during your meditation times.

Sometimes you may find yourself expecting too much too soon from your meditation practice. Letting go of your expectations and what you should expect to happen. Simply go with the flow of where your meditation exercises take you. Find enjoyment in how you feel when you are preparing, during and after your practice. Keep a journal of your journey as you continue through the meditation so that you are able to gauge what benefits you are seeing. Find happiness in the new way that you are living your life.

When you are just beginning with meditation, it is easy to believe that you must have complete silence. However, this is not the case. In fact, if you start your meditation practices in complete silence, you will find that you are going to get distracted very easily by outside noises that you cannot control.

Instead, be more concerned with finding a space that you are comfortable. When the sounds in your environment come up randomly, treat them like you thoughts, notice them and do not get involved. It does take some practice. Over time, you will be able to hear noises during your meditation and not be distracted away from your breathing. If you are having an especially difficult time concentrating, you can use noise canceling headphones, but you will need to eventually work your way to meditating when there is background noise.

Letting go of the stereotype that meditation is only for spiritual people, a new age idea or for tree huggers. In fact, there are people from all walks of life and age young and old who practice meditation. Of course it can have a religious focus, but this is not necessary for meditation practice. Another misconception is that is has to be a serious matter with saying mantras of "om" and sitting cross legged. This is an idea that can be incorporated if you wish, but it is not necessary. So perform your meditation practice how you feel comfortable, no matter if you are 2 or 102 years old.

It can be an easy task to start something new because it can be an exciting experience. However, the trick is sticking with it when the novelty wears off. This happens because many of the meditation practices can feel repetitive. Remind yourself that you are training your mind to shift perspective on the way that you view your feelings and thoughts.

One main reason why people throw in the towel is that they do not feel like their mind is clear or empty. It simply is not working! However, like with all things that are worth achieving, there is a level of dedication and perseverance that is required so that you can push past this phase. Remember that the mind is programmed to think. Meditation is not a magical potion so that it will make your thoughts disappear completely. However, you need to learn, practice and master meditation, and the only way you are able to achieve this is to continue to build your habit of meditation.

Some are very excited about trying out a different technique each time they sit down to meditate. This is alright for a short time as you are beginning and finding the technique that resonates best with you. However, if you are continuously switching between methods, you are not going to gain the full benefits of the particular meditation you are performing.

Above all, make your meditation practice a part of your day that you look forward to. It is your way of keeping your mind balanced throughout the rest of the day, and you will help to keep you more focused and aware. Trust me, when you are able to keep up with your practices, you will start to see the benefits that ripple throughout your life. Then you will be wanting to share this secret with everyone.

Chapter 2: Introduction to Reiki

Reiki is an ancient technique which was created in Japan which centers around healing, stress reduction and relaxation. It is derived from two Japanese words. *Rei* means *higher power where Ki* has the meaning of *life force energy.* In full, the word Reiki means *spiritually guided life force energy.*

You practice Reiki methods by hovering your hands or lightly laying your hands in a particular area of the body to promote healing. It manipulates and transmutes the energy that is found within the body known as Chi, Shakti or Life Force. You are able to build energy if it is too low and lower it if it should be too high.

Reiki does not just revolve around the energies within the body. It has an effect on you as an entire person, encompassing the spirit, mind, emotions and the body in the treatment. You may find many benefits such as overall well being, security, peace and relaxation. In some instances, there are people who experience miraculous results. Any individual is able to use Reiki because it is not base on spiritual development of intellectual capacity.

Even though Reiki is spiritually based, it is not a religion. There is no dogma attached and you do not need to hold particular beliefs to use Reiki. In fact, Reiki will work even if you do not have a belief in the practice itself, although, it would be more powerful if you do believe that it will work for you.

Using the techniques and intention of Reiki to heal and balance your body, you will be able to help your body to heal from different illnesses. It is believed that energy is blocked and cannot flow properly resulting in illness. When this blockage is removed, you will be able to treat the illness in a more direct way than with conventional medicine. You will find with the chakra meditations that you are able to utilize this transfer of energy to heal your energy centers of the body, resulting in lasting effects felt throughout your body on a physical, mental and spiritual level.

Health Benefits of Reiki

Overall, Reiki manipulates the movement of the life force energy within the body. You will be able to realize many physical and emotional benefits to include the following:

- aids relaxation
- assists in the natural healing process
- hightens spiritual, mental and emotional well being
- helps with coping with difficulties
- relieves emotional stress

From a medical standpoint, Reiki has been successfully used to treat and sometimes cure:

- Fatigue syndromes

- Crohn's disease

- Autism

- Neurodegenerative disorders

- Infertility

- Chronic pain

- Depression

- Anxiety

- Heart Disease

- Cancer

- Stress

Reiki Healing for Anxiety & Stress

Anxiety and Stress are the most experienced medical conditions which are seen in modern society. Reiki healing can be a huge benefit to relieving the symptoms of these experiences. Let us go over the basics of these two conditions so that you can realize if you have problems with them and how reiki and meditation can help you in these cases.

Anxiety

Having occasional experiences of anxiety is a normal fact of life. However, if you are having issues with anxiety that are affecting your daily life, this is known as an anxiety disorder. This is where you are experiencing frequent amounts of persistent and excessive worry which is intense. They can involve repeated occurrence of sudden feelings, and they can also result in panic attacks which are fear, torror and intense anxiety about a particular situation.

These anxiety disorders can start to develop as early as childhood or teenage years and continue to strengthen in intensity during your adulthood. You may start to revolve your day avoid particular places or people so that you do not trigger your emotions. The common disorders of anxiety are known as generalized anxiety disorder, social anxiety disorder and separation anxiety disorder. You are able to have two of these anxiety orders simultaneously.

Common Symptoms of Anxiety

From the wide range of anxiety disorders, the most common symptoms are:

- difficulty controlling worry – this is the symptom experienced the most. It is categorized by the worry being disproportionate to the situations that trigger the worry. Usually it is connected with everyday situations. To be diagnosed with generalized anxiety disorder, you must have frequent occurrences of uncontrollable worry over the course of six months.

- difficulty sleeping – Disturbances in sleep are highly associated with anxiety disorders. This can include a wide range such as waking up in the middle of the night, difficulty falling asleep and insomnia. It is unclear what the link is between anxiety and sleeping disorders. However when the anxiety disorder is treated and under control, the sleep issues improve as well.

- trouble with concentration – This is a heavy hitter when it comes to anxiety disorders. More than 2/3 percent of the people suffering from anxiety disorders have issues with focus, short term memory and concentration. Even with this large number, it is not a surefire way of knowing you have issues with anxiety.

- overactive or feeling tired – Even though this can be a symptom for a wide range of disorders, becoming easily fatigued is a red flag for doctors when discussing anxiety disorders. Because of this reason, this symptom alone is not able to lead a doctor to a diagnosis of anxiety disorder. Alternatively, you can also experience the opposite of having hyperactivity. Fatigue is more tricky as it can be an occurrence experienced only after panic attacks or it can be chronic and experienced throughout the day.

- hyperventilation or rapid breathing – Panic attacks happen when you are under an immense amount of worry, and this leads to you not being able to physically be able to breath without hyperventilating. It is due to an intense amount of fear and can be a debilitating experience. Panic attacks usually have fear of dying, nausea, chest tightness, shaking and sweating that occur with the rapid breathing. They must occur frequently to be deemed as worthy of a diagnosis.

- feeling agitated – When anxiety hits a person, their sympathetic nervous system is sent into overdrive. With this effect, it causes a ripple effect throughout the body, resulting in symptoms of dry mouth, shaky hands, sweaty palms and a racing heart. This is in response to your brain believing that you are in danger

- overall feeling of tension, restlessness or nervousness – This is a symptom seen mainly in teens and children. It is categorized by the individual feeling like they are on edge or experiencing an uncomfortable urge to move. Even though it is a symptom that is not found in each patient, it is one of the indicating symptoms that doctors look for before diagnosis.

Causes of Anxiety Disorders

There are many causes of anxiety disorders that are not fully understood because it affects each individual on a personal level. Traumatic life experiences are going to affect people in different ways. It is thought that inherited personality traits may also be a cause of people being more sensitive to anxiety issues.

For others, underlying medical issues can be to blame as the cause for anxiety disorders. In fact, seeing signs of anxiety usually triggers an investigation which brings these medical conditions to light. Here is a list of common medical issues which are seen in conjunction with anxiety disorders.

- Chronic pain

- Irritable bowel syndrome

- Withdrawal from medications or alcohol

- Misuse of drug or withdrawal

- COPD or asthma

- Hyperthyroidism

- Diabetes

- Heart disease

You can also be at increased risk of having an anxiety disorder if you have issues with one or more of the following:

- Alcohol or drugs

- Having a family history of anxiety disorders in blood relatives

- Other mental health disorders such as depression

- Buildup of stress due to illness or a death in the family

- Trauma

Stress

Stress is very common today, and it is an emotional or physical response to pressures or demands that are experienced daily. Stress can be a positive part of life when experienced in small doses. It is able to help people to take action, be stimulated, develop and to grow. However, if you are experiencing high levels of stress frequently, it can be due to an imbalance in lifestyle and can include any area of your life such as illness, relationships, money and/or work.

Common Symptoms of Stress

When you having issues with prolonged stress, your symptoms can include one or more of the following:

- Irritability
- Difficulty with making decisions
- Difficulty relaxing
- Depression
- Lowered confidence levels
- Difficulty concentrating
- Sleep disturbances
- Difficulty breathing
- Decreased sexual function or libido
- Appetite changes
- Muscle spasms or nervous twitches
- Headaches
- Low energy levels
- Muscle pain and spasms
- High blood pressure
- Hyperventilation
- Heart palpitations
- Gastrointestinal issues such as irritable bowel syndrome, heartburn and indigestion
- Anxiety
- Autoimmune diseases
- Withdrawal from others
- Procrastinating or neglecting responsibilities

Causes of Stress

There are many levels of causes which can lead to stress. Most of them are extreme changes to our normal day routine. External causes of stress include the following:

- Children and family members
- Having too busy of a schedule
- Financial issues
- Romantic relationship difficulties
- School or work
- Major life changes

Internal causes of stress are the following:

- All or nothing attitude
- Perfectionism or unrealistic expectations
- Negative self-talk
- Lack of flexibility or rigid thinking
- Inability to accept uncertainty
- Pessimism

The most common life events which can cause undue stress are the following:

- Retirement
- Marriage reconciliation
- Job loss

- Marriage
- Illness or injury
- Death of a close family member
- Imprisonment
- Separation in a romantic relationship
- Divorce
- Death of a spouse or partner

These causes can lead to results or symptoms in our life that rise in a physical way. Some examples are:

- acne – This is likely the most visible way that stress reveils itself. This is due to people touching their face more often when they are stressed which leads to the spread of bacteria and the appearance of acne.

- headaches – Stress can lead to pain within the head as well as the neck. This happens in over 50% of people who experience undue stress in their lives. The pain can range in intensity and can even be debilitating.

- frequent illness – Having heightened levels of stress lowers the immune system effectiveness leading you to feel sick more often than if you did not have undue stress in your life. This leads to illnesses ranging from a runny nose to the flu. However, be sure to look at your physical exercises level and your diet to see if they are to blame first.

How Reiki Can Help

In general, Reiki helps a person to feel more calm and centered. They are able to take back control of their lives without the use of expensive doctors and treatments. In fact, you are able to use these tactics yourself, so you can heal your body when you feel out of balance. Being able to use the healing energy work of Reiki helps own to feel more in control and more confident.

Anxiety and stress symptoms are able to be dealt with on a personal level which is unique to the individual. Since both of these diagnosis stems from personal perspectives on life's events, it is important to approach the healing in a very personal way. Reiki and meditation are able to help you do just that.

As for the physical symptoms that can be experienced, being able to calm down the and make the energy flow properly throughout your body, the ripple effect is going to come down to changes in your body physically. Many of the physical symptoms of stress and anxiety are going to be erased due to the correct energy flow.

Being able to balance out the energy flowing through your chakras, it also reduces the response from the brain to go into flight or fight mode. When you are more calm and centered, you will be able to think more clearly and feel more vibrant.

In fact, more and more private practices, hospice and hospitals are incorporating Reiki sessions coupled with modern medicine. There have been many patients who have reported that they had a reduction in their symptoms, which makes it a beneficial approach to those suffering from anxiety and stress.

So Why 21 Days of Reiki?

There is an intense amount of cleansing that is occurring in the body during this process of healing. You need to ensure that you are drinking enough water and getting a sufficient amount of sleep so that your body is able to cleanse more efficiently. When you work with the meditations, you are also going to be clearing out negative energies and toxins that have built up over your lifetime. There are 7 main chakras which are worked with, and each chakra has 3 days of practice.

With the amount of new energy that is being channeled into the body, it takes a course of 21 days for your body to adjust and adapt to the new activity. From a psychological standpoint, it takes approximately 21 days for a person to form a new habit.

Even though stress is put upon the first 21 days of starting Reiki, this does not mean that the process is complete after this time. It is very important to keep up the practices so that you able to reap the best results from practicing Reiki.

Continuing to practice daily is a way to ensure that you do not have a build up of germs, emotions, negative thoughts or negativity in your life. You do not realize how much of these you pick up on a subconscious level each day. Being able to address these issues on a daily basis helps keep them at a minimum while you are reaping the benefits of living a balanced and healthy life.

Not only does daily practice keep these aspects in balance, it helps you to build up energy that has been lost throughout the day. As you continue the practice, you will continue to clear out your chakras which will lead you to see the full benefits of Reiki practice over time. Even though this book focuses on the first 21 days, it is important to keep up the practice for a minimum of 3 months so that you can see the true effects that the Reiki has on your body, mind and spirit.

Chapter 3 - Introduction to Psychic Abilities

Even though you may be unaware, every person is capable of tapping into their psychic abilities. This is because we are all immortal and infinite beings of energy and is comprised of a part of the universe known as your soul. Most of us have been conditioned to believe that intuitive and psychic abilities are not actually true because there are many charlatans out there that take advantage of people with their "powers" better known as deceptions. Using a trick of the mind for people who are desperate or in need is a powerful tool that they are able to use to their own advantage. Because of the encounters with these people in the media or in real life, society as a whole are sceptical of psychic ability's existence.

A good example is when you were a child, you may have had more psychic encounters. Children are more in touch with the energies around them, and they are more pure from the experiences of life. As a result, you likely were able to hear, dream or sense otherworldly energies or words. Because society has been conditioned to believe that psychic connections are not real, the adults in your life likely shrugged off your experiences or explained them away in a logical fashion.

However, there are some people who are fortunate enough to be able to learn about these abilities from their family members or other caretakers. These are the people that have a solid belief that there rare other energies that exist outside of ourselves, and they will support and teach the connected child so that they are better equipped to deal with all of the rare occurrences that most people will consider them crazy.

As an example, you may have had an experience with communicating with a spirit or ghost who was not there in physical form, but you were able to see and play with them as if they were real. If you confide in your parents about this person, they likely were not able to see this spirit themselves, so instead of taking you at your word, they explain it by saying that you have an imaginary friend. This is a more accepted belief in society, although far fetched for some, but most people will not think the child is crazy for making up a friend to spend their time with.

Because this experience was not defined in the proper way, you yourself most likely started to believe that this spirit was all part of your imagination as well – that you created it in your mind. However, it is very likely that you were able to see what other people could not see because of your innocence and overall trusting of the world. The magic that is experienced in the world through the eyes of a child is lost usually as you get older and start to get bogged down with tragic and emotional occurrences ranging from love to working at a job. These are not part of a child's life, and therefore, their soul is more clean for these higher energies to come through more easily.

Even if you have lost this connection as you become an adult, this does not mean this skill is forever lost. In fact, any person of any age is able to practice and work to strengthen their psychic abilities, and it requires an ample amount of self-love, exercise and patience. One of the main ways to achieve this is to switch your perspective that these abilities are a form of deception or falsehood. They are nothing of the sort, and you do not need to rely on what society has conditioned you to think through the media.

When you tap into your psychic skills, you are going to have heightened sensitivity to one or a combination of your taste, sense, feeling, hearing, vision and intuition of the energetic world. In fact in the science of psychology, there is no true definition as to how to define "normal" and as such, it is a personal scale that you base this upon. With these heightened perceptions, there are many levels of intensities. As you begin to get back in touch with your intuition and psychic abilities, you will find that the intensity will strengthen the more that you practice.

It is important to mention since you will be perceiving the world from a different perspective that you may feel more alienated as you will not be able to talk to just anybody about your personal experiences. However, there are many people just like you who have been practicing for various amounts of time that you will be able to confide in and even receive insight or guidance. Being able to tap into these extra sensory sides of ourselves, you will gain a better understanding of yourself and the world around you. The deeper you go, the most surreal your experiences to the point where you may find it difficult to put them into words. This is all part of the experience as you deepen your connection with yourself and the energies of the other worlds.

Connecting with your Intuition Again

When you are starting to work on your psychic abilities, it is imperative that you have a bond with your intuition. This relationship is going to strengthen and deepen over time as you learn to trust and truly listen to what your senses are telling you. You will start to notice the messages that your body is giving you through your intuition when you know the signs. You will need to pay close attention as we can hear a voice in our minds that we label as intuition, but it can be your ego trying to trick you that it is okay to do what you ultimately wanted to do in the first place.

One way to practice getting back in touch or strengthening your intuition is to create a visualization. See yourself a coffee shop sharing a drink with an old childhood friend that you have not seen since you were a child. You take the time to catch up on your experiences and go over all of the old stories that you shared together during your childhood. Through these conversations, you are able to remember the dynamic of the personal relationship that you had with them all this time ago, but it feels as if you had not spent so much time apart.

Even so, you feel a distance because of your different experiences you both have had and feel that you are strangers in this regard. To be able to take away this feeling of alienation, you would need to get to know your friend again as they are now instead of who they were in your memory.

This is the same way that you need to approach your intuition as if it was your old childhood friend. In this perspective, you are able to see that your intuition has always been a part of you, but you may have taken different routes and not kept in touch. However, it is always possible to rekindle this relationship with your intuition once again. Being able to take the time each day to work on this relationship just like you would with any other person, you will find that you will be able to cultivate this connection is a very personal way.

Intuition Building Exercises

To perform this exercise, you will need to evaluate your emotions and associate a color with each emotion. You can use the typical color representations such as blue meaning healing energy or red meaning angry. However, you need to pick a color scheme that resonates best with you for this exercise.

Start this practice by thinking of a situation which is straightforward, such as a text message with a potential partner or lover. You may have thoughts of love or disdain for this person. Depending on your personal feelings about this situation, assign a color to the feelings of love or disdain which may be pink or red for love and a more negative color such as black or purple for disdain. Remember there is no wrong color choice and you must choose the color that you personally would associate with your feelings.

During future interactions with this emotion and person, you will start to rewire your energy to associate this color with this particular emotion. Through this exercise, you will be able to strengthen your intuition by the color association and you will be able to communicate with your intuition nonverbally through these emotion based colors. Over time, your intuition is going to be more in tune with these color schemes and be able to signal to you through colors so that you can see the bigger picture of a situation.

As an example, if you associated love with red, when your friend is talking about a specific person, and you are able to see the color red while she is talking about them, you will intuitively know that there is a loving connection between the two without your friend needing to express this directly.

Another practice is scanning a room so that you are able to get a feel for your current environment. This is done while you have positioned yourself in the center of a room which does not have other people there. You can choose to move around the energy of the space through the movement of your eyes to witness what is going on or you can physically move about the room. Take mental notes of the scents, sounds and sights that you are taking in. Ask yourself where you are being pulled to energetically and people and places that you feel like you should avoid. Be as detailed as possible by examining the furniture, windows and corners of this space and how they make you feel internally.

The more that you practice this exercise, you will be able to do this same practice in a room of people. This is a more intense version of the exercise, and may be intense the first time depending on your level of sensitivity. Listen to your body and cease if it should become too much. However, do not let these feelings of anxiousness divert you from developing your skills. There are going to be growing pains and tests along the way, but once you push through these feelings, great benefits await you on the other side.

You can also use this exercise in other places such as subways, offices, bars and parks. Being able to practice this technique in common areas that you frequent will help you to become more familiar with the energies of your surrounds and continue to solidify your relationship with your intuition.

Another exercise that you can practice is using the subconscious and your dreams. It is through your dreams that you are able to digest and absorb the energies that you come in contact with during the day that have not been particularly resolved. Since we are not able to live balanced and healthy lives by absorbing every instance that we encounter in a single day, our psyche comes into play to help us to find that balance that is required for a functional and healthy lifestyle.

Through dream work, you are able to remove the constraints of this physical plane where you are able to effortlessly move throughout spaces and other planes. It is rather common to encounter spirits of other realms, travel into the future as well as the past or explore foreign lands. There is no limit to where you can go in the subconscious which makes it an endless pool of possibilities to discover.

To be able to get the most of the knowledge that you gain through your dreams, be sure to keep a journal and pen next to your bed. It is all too common that you forget these adventures and information gathered in the dream world. You can curb this tendency by creating a habit of writing down what you remember the moment that you wake. This way it is fresh in your mind. Even if you only remember one part of your dream, write it down. You may find that you are able to remember other parts of your dreams as you writing down the one part that you remembered upon waking.

This is a daily practice which can also be used throughout the day. Strengthening your intuition requires that you are mindful of the people you surround yourself with. Make sure that you trust the people who are in your inner circle and that they are positive minded. Eliminate energy vampires out of your life if at all possible. Notice your levels of intuition while you are around certain people. If it is being strengthen while interacting with them, spend more time with them whenever possible. Guard the strength of your intuition by steering away from people who drain you, especially as you are working on building your skill.

Test your intuitive skills with your close friends by asking them about specific tips and information in which you are receiving. This will help guide you to trust your intuitive skills more when they confirm that your feelings and sensitivities are correct. As you deepen your trust in your intuition, you will learn to rely on it more fully and in effect it will strengthen.

Now that you have the basis to help you out with your daily self-care measures, you will be more ready to take on the challenges of fortifying your intuitive skills. Let us explore the other ways that you can strengthen your personal talents.

Set Challenges for Yourself

Set personal goals for yourself to continue to push yourself to your limits. Think outside of the box and expand your personal talents. This does not have to include sensitive matters. Examples include learning a foreign language, taking up a new hobby or even learning how to play a musical instrument.

This will continue to broaden your horizons, help you to come in contact with different types of people and strengthen your body and mind. This is turn will help you with your intuitive talents as you will be utilizing them to learn new things. You will also be humbled as you continue to learn and hone your skills. When you are in a humbled state, you become more empathetic and grateful.

While you are in position of challenge, these are times where you will learn more about yourself and how you interact with the world around you. You will grow in ways that you would not have without the challenge in place and end up being grateful for the experiences.

Get out of Your Comfort Zone

When you are put into new situations, it makes you rely more on your intuitive skills to help you navigate through unknown areas. Travel is especially a great way in doing this. Not only will you learn about new places, but you will come in contact with different cultures than your own. This will help to broaden your ideas and thoughts.

It will also help you to understand more types of people which will come in handy as it will aid you in helping different kinds of people. Gratefulness for the uniqueness of people will arise. Your listening skills will also be honed as you learn more about the new places and people. When you are forced to see situations in a different light, it sparks your creativity to find a solution to situations. This may help to broaden your problem solving skills while learning about new things in the process.

This will force you as well to squash any fear of the unknown. This fear is debilitating and unfounded. It is simply that you do not know what to expect that you have fear about doing certain things. However, nine times out of ten after getting through new situations, you will be better for it, and that fear will no longer exist. The less fear you have, the more you are able to thrive with your psychic skills.

Walk in Other People's Shoes

When you are able to take yourself out of the situation, it will make you a better listener and hone your intuitive skills. This forces you to place yourself in their position while thinking about what you would do in those same situations given their circumstances.

Practicing this exercise has multi levels of understanding about people. First off, it will help you to see situations from different perspectives while you are learning about their experiences. Another benefit is that you will likely be less judgmental as you will have a deeper knowledge of this person and in turn others.

At the end of the day, you will realize that each person who walks this earth has problems. No one is exempt from this fact and many times there are problems which go on for quite some time be it from complication or ignoring the fact. This may help you also to feel more grateful for the problems that you have, and, perhaps, they are not as bad as you had thought before.

As an added bonus, walking in another's shoes helps you to become more patient. Sometimes talking about issues can be challenging or it may be a complex issue which is complicated to put into words. As this person is possibly mustering up the courage and know how to express their story, you will become patient as you try to understand better what they are going through.

Find your Kindred Spirits

Many times, psychic people may feel isolated from their family members or other people who they come in contact with daily. However, it is very likely that you will have another family member who has the same talents as you. They will be a great guide in asking for the methods that they use to strengthen their own intuitive skills. They can also help you along with issues that you are experiencing as they have most likely gone through the same situation or something similar.

Also, other people who are in a deeper connection with their intuition are able to sense each other. You will likely be drawn to many of them as they will be towards you. When you create a network of people who you can relate to, this not only makes you feel more secure in being an intuitive, but it gives you a support system which is much needed. You will be able to help each other to keep you on the straight and narrow as they will let you know if you seem off or give you techniques to strengthen your skills that had worked for them.

Analyze your Thoughts and Beliefs

Take a long hard look the basis for your beliefs and thoughts as these are going to create the environment within and without you. This includes anything that needs obvious attention such as recurring cycles of unlearned lessons as well as more hidden aspects of yourself. This is the time to be honest with yourself. Only then will you be able to deepen your relationship not only with yourself but with others around you.

When you have predetermined biases and beliefs which have no foundation, this direct affects how you deal with other people. Once these issues are faced head on, you will be able to help others on a more connected nature. It will also aid you in being able to be even more objective about situations.

If you are having issues with finding items which need attention, make a point to dig deeper. We all have biases whether they are based in gender, race or age. We are all unique creatures with special characteristics that we bring to the table. Take this opportunity to learn and to grow, and it will strengthen your empathy even further.

Take this opportunity to let go of negative thoughts, feelings and beliefs which are no longer serving you. Any sort of negativity is going to impede your attitude and growth. When you are harboring these negative thoughts, you are affecting your environment even down the neurochemical level which affects your organs, overall body, your mental attitude and bleeds into your outer environment.

Keep a Curious Mind

Remember when you were a child and you could not satiate your curiosity about everything? This is the mental attitude you need to continue to possess as you grow into adulthood. There is always something to learn. Once you think you know it all, you need to take a step back. Even for talents that you already possess, there is always something that can be perfected or learned about.

There are also other instances where this will come in handy when dealing with people from different walks of life. Perhaps you are dealing with someone who has an unfaltering view which you think is narrow. Or maybe you assume that your green co-worker certain has no knowledge about life. How are you so sure until you ask and dig deeper?

Everyone grows up in different situations and sees the world with a perspective in which you probably do not share. When you delve into learning about these curiosities within other people, you will also look at yourself in a new light. It will in turn help you to understand people better.

Deepen Your Understanding

The best way to understand people better is to ask better thought out questions. The questions which bring about the most interesting insights are intellectual or even provocative. When we talk about the issues in which most people do not bring up in daily interactions, we will learn more as well as see this person perhaps in a different light.

You can practice this with family members, clients or colleagues. Not only will these conversations strengthen your relationship with them, it will give you a broader insight into people from all walks of life. The key is to never think you are ever done with improving yourself or your intuitive skills.

Become more Aware of the Details

There is no doubt that when an intuitive becomes more in tune with the environment within themselves and around them that they are able to pick up on more cues which will aid in becoming even deeply connected. There are a few ways in which someone can foster this exercise.

Firstly, you can sit in a room by yourself. This can be a place that you frequent or a totally new place. Sit quietly without any distractions and take in all the details of the space. Even if you think you know every aspect of your familiar space, make a point to look for the less obvious things. This will train your eye to keep open to new occurrences or even shifts in energy.

Another way is to come up with a mental picture in your mind which is not complex. It can be as simple as a small colored dot or a shape which is in 2D. When first starting out, try to keep your mind focused on this object for at least fifteen seconds or longer if you are able. This will train your mind to not run through so many thoughts, to slow down and to also become more present in the moment.

As you are able to consistently keep this image in your mind for the fifteen second increment, start to add form to your shape, creating a 3D object. To further escalate the exercise, start to rotate the object in your mind's eye and add more detail. Once this accomplished, set your time limit to half a minute.

The point of this exercise is to train your eyes to extract more information from your world around you. After dedicated practice, you will be able to gather details extremely quickly which will assist you in reading people and environments. It may also help you in situations where you are going to need to think very fast.

Focus on your Emotions

You can practice this same idea while focusing on a certain emotion within your heart. This exercise will not even improve your intuitive abilities; it will continue to keep positive emotion in your heart throughout the day while building your institution.

With this technique, you need to feel a deep positive emotion such as affection, joy, kindness, appreciation or love. This emotion is going to consume you first through your whole heart and then vibrate through your mind and body. It will be more powerful if you associate a bright light with this emotion so that you can both visualize and feel this emotion reverberate throughout your body.

Just like the focus exercise, you want to hold this feeling for as long as possible without getting distracted. Put all your energy and focus into this exercise so that it is more impactful. Not only will it strengthen your energy from the inside out, it will develop your visualization skills.

This is also a skill that you will need to develop if you come in contact with energy vampires, narcissists or overall negative people. When this exercise is done around these people, they will likely be aware on the outside. However, you are putting up a barrier so that they are not able to siphon your energy from you.

Deepen Your Objectiveness

When you are objective, you are free of bias and look at all the details in front of you to make a decision or to counsel someone. When you are able to listen from multiple points of view, objectiveness will come to you naturally. To strengthen this skill, you will need to be in contact with people who have different views from your own. Even if they do not think the same way that you do, it does not necessarily mean that they are taking a negative stance. Even knowing the negative side will help you to understand the full spectrum of the situation.

If you have a strong belief about a certain issue such as motorcycle safety for instance, you need to speak to motorcyclists who do not believe in wearing helmets or full protective gear. They may have a different experience than you have which will help you to see the entire picture. This will also break down your judgments of people and help you understand and perceive emotions from different types of people other than who you may be comfortable with.

Listen to Inner Guidance

The best way to strengthen your intuition is to go to the source. Your intuition is that inner voice which is in all people. The sensitive empaths have a fast track to communicating with this inner voice. It is your intuition which has all the answers that you need about your personal growth and healing. This inner voice is always going to lead you to your highest good. It will never make you feel negative feelings and only has love and compassion for you.

The only way to tap into this higher level of intuition is to quiet your mind and clear out what you think you already know. This inner voice can only be heard clearly when all of this clutter is out of the way. This can be done through several methods to include:

- Simply being silent in a space which is also quiet

- Meditation

- Prayer or Mantras

- Connecting with Nature

When you practice one of the methods at least five minutes a day, you will start to tap into your institution more deeply. This may appear as an epiphany, memory, sound, image, hunch or gut feeling. Those who continue to practice may actually hear their inner voice. When any of these signs make themselves known, you need to acknowledge them. It may also be wise to jot them down in a notebook so that you can expand on this knowledge that you gain at a later time.

Pay Attention to Your Dreams

Dreams are a source of intuition, and they need to have attention paid to them. During REM sleep which occurs approximately every ninety minutes each time you sleep, this is the time that dreams are experienced. These dreams can be excellent guides to show us direction in career choices, relationship, and health among others. The trick is remembering them.

The best way to do this is to keep a dream notebook by your bed. The best time to write is the moment that you wake up because you will remember the most at this time. You may even remember more of the dream as you are writing. When you make a habit of writing down your dreams, this process will become a habit, and it will become much easier to recall the dreams.

If you need some insight on a particular issue, ask a question before going to sleep. Like usual, write down any dreams that you remember, even if it does not seem to answer your question. Each night, ask the same question until you get a more solid answer to your inquiry.

Write It Down

Many times it gets very confusing in an empath's mind, especially when there are many other people's emotions and feelings wrapped up in their own. When you utilize writing down these thoughts that run through your mind, you are able to start deciphering what you are actually feeling compared to the other emotions that you are experiencing.

Not only will this help to raise your awareness, it will also help you to realize when you are soaking up people's energies when you do not intend to. The moment that you start to feel something different than what is true to you personally, you can stop the flow of energy or excuse yourself from this person's presence if possible.

Psychic Skill Development

When you have strengthened your intuition, you will be able to efficiently practice your psychic skill development.

There are many different types of psychic abilities of which I will go over a few in detail. It is possible to have one or a combination of these skills, and to have different intensities of each skill that you can further develop if you wish.

The Basics of Telekinesis

The ability of telekinesis, also known as Psychokinesis, has a certain mysitcal air as you will see this abilitiy in frequently in a sci-fi or horror movie. This is the ability to move or manipulate objects solely with your mind. Psychokinesis is translated from Greek words for motion and mind.

When you view everything in this world and the other planes based in a vibration of energy, you will be more effective in honing your psychic abilities. Items that we see as solid matter are more dense energies where as pure energies that you see and feel are lighter energies with a higher vibration point. When you are using this perspective to work on your telekinesis skills, you will be able to perceive this energy on a personal level and, through practice, be able to manipulate it with the power of your mind.

A summary of the different components of telekinesis is as follows:

❖ Relaxation is required so that you are able to disconnect your body and mind from the every day things that you usually process. When you are able to accomplish this task, you will be in a state of consciousness that you are able to focus and expand upon your thought processes.

❖ Concentration is also a required element as it is ultimately your will that will help you to be successful at manipulating these energies.

❖ Meditation is a process which will help your mind to accomplish both relaxation and concentration as you practice any exercise to hone your psychic abilities.

❖ Gratitude is the final component which will help you to strengthen your connection to the energies outside of yourself. When you are able to demonstrate any of your psychic skills, it is due to the universe for giving you these capabilities, and respect needs to be paid to these energies.

While you are practicing the telekinesis exercises, or any of the psychic skill exercises, you need to have a firm belief that these are very real abilities. When this is in place, no matter the outcome of your exercises, you know that the result was meant to be at that time. You are not always going to be successful, and that is perfectly okay. You are only trying to get back into connection with who you are internally, and there is no wrong way of following this path.

As you continue to practice your psychic exercises and gain some control over them, there will be naysayers who are going to make it their mission that you are crazy for following this dream and that they do not exist. Acknowledge what they are saying, but fall back on your ultimate belief in what you are pursuing.

Recognize that we are all at different levels of development in this soul journey. There is no point in arguing over matters of opinion with a person who is not a master at these skills. Remember, society has molded us into holding these beliefs. If you believe differently, you have this right. At the end of the day, you need to live your life how you see fit, and many people before you have done these same practices with the same goal in mind. Keep an open mind during the exercises, and prepare yourself to be amazed.

Logically thinking about this skill is going to bring about visions of you sitting in your favorite and comfortable chair as you use the power of your mind to bring you everything that you wish. However, telekinesis does not work in this way. When you have mastered the art of telekinesis, you will be able to manipulate small objects.

You must think in terms of energy. It takes an extreme amount of concentration, dedication and practice to be able to strengthen this skill, just to make small amounts of changes. Because of this fact, you are not able to move larger items such as a car or an elephant because of the sheer amount of will power and energy that it requires.

Because of this fact, scientific studies have focused on small and mundane feats such as testing the ability versus probability of a pair of dice landing on a certain number or having an effect on a computerized random number generator. The tests also rely more on complicated analyses of statistics. That is to say, scientists are less interested if a person is able to knock a glass over or bend a spoon. Rather, they would rather test if a person is able to control a coin coming up on tails at a significantly higher percentage than 50%.

Exercises to Develop your Telekinesis

Even with scientific studies resulting in mixed conclusions, there are many people who work at perfecting this skill. While you are practicing these exercises, you must have no doubt in your mind, even on a subconscious level, that you are going to be able to perform telekinesis. You will need to couple your meditations with visualizing exercises.

When you have gotten to the point where you have your mind cleared, select a small and simple object in your surrounding environment and study it so that you are aware of its every detail. Pay special attention to the scent, how soft or hard the object is, color and shape.

After some time of perfecting your visualization skills, close your eyes and visualize your object with every detail you studied. Create a connection by focusing all of your attention to your visualization of this object. Start to make the object move in your visualization how you would like to have the object moved in the physical plane.

Then you will transfer this same energy and intention towards the object in the physical plane. This is best performed by looking at the space between you and the object, then you want to take this space away. Envision you and this object as one with no separation in between.

For the objects that you want to move, it is best to start with something simple such as a matchstick or a pencil. When you are able to successfully move these items, move up to more complicated items such as a glass or lighter.

Continue to practice daily until you start to see results while refining your abilities each time. Over time, hone your visualization skills by expanding the objects that you are envisioning. Step up the objects by complexity and details. After some time of practicing, you can visualize an entire room. The focus of your visualization practices should be getting the visions as detailed as possible.

A specialized meditation practice that you can use is to sit in a comfortable position. After taking a few regular breaths, breathe in deeply for a count of 4. Hold your breath for another count of 4. Then exhale through your mouth for 8 seconds.

After a series of 3 rounds of breath have been completed, let each thought that comes across transform into a sparkle in your field of visualization as you are breathing inwards and while you are holding your breath. As you exhale, allow those sparkles to become one as bright as the sun. Repeat this process as much as necessary until you are finished with your designated meditation time. This exercise will help with both your focus and your visualization skills.

You can also work with your skills by manipulating a candle flame. Light a candle and perform your meditation exercise. Gaze at the flame and let it take over your thoughts. Watch intently and take note when the flame flickers and moves. After your mind is solely concentrated on the flame, try to manipulate which way the flame is going to move with your focused energy.

First move the flame to the left and then to the right. Then try to make the flame grow larger, then make the flame brighter and finally work on having the flame diminish.

With the practice of any of these exercises, you need to stop when you are physically or mental drained. Taking regular breaks if you are extensively practicing is important. Take at least a few hours break if you become tired during these exercises. Make sure that you drink enough water and eat a small snack to keep your energy levels risen. Even if you need a longer break, do not go back to practicing until you are feeling revived in mind and body.

The Basics of Pyrokinesis

Fire is an element which has an underlying fearsome factor, but it is also well known to garnish an impactful amount of power. It was because of fire that the cavemen were able to rise in the food chain above the animals. Likewise, fire can cause a great deal of destruction and hurt. Being able to control the element of fire is the main concept of pyrokinesis.

Pyrokinesis is derived from the Greek word pyro, or fire, and kinesis which is movement. A person who hones this skill is able to manipulate as well as create fires simply by the power of their mind. They do not use any substances to be able to create these flames. Pyrokinesis is a subset of telekinesis because people who are adept at these two practices are able to manipulate the world around them.

As an example of the skill, you can light a stack of paperwork on the floor in the living room. A master at pyrokinesis is able to light this fire with their mind. They will also be able to control that fire so that it will only continue to burn the paper and nothing else or they can dictate the direction in which the fire is going to burn and cause the whole house to burn down if they wish.

There have been no scientific tests to prove the validity of pyrokinesis, but this practice has been practiced with a handful of martial arts practitioners. These masters are able to transform their chi energy so that the heat can be felt in the areas that they choose.

Episodes of spontaneous combustion have also been recorded as far back as 1763. This is where the body of a person catches on fire without any fuel to ignite the fire. This can result in the body smoking and well as the formation of blisters and burns. Others will catch on fire completely, and is seen surprisingly in older people more often. For the firefighters who are familiar with victims of fires, they know that the injuries sustained the typical markers of a fire victim is that their trunk is usually whole while the head and limbs are incarcerated.

However, for the spontaneous combustion cases, it is the opposite with the trunk of the body being nearly gone while the feet and hands remain. It is also a curious case because the flammable items around the body will be in tact with no signs of burning. This makes those who are familiar with spontaneous combustion cases that these fires started from within the truck of their body.

Even though spontaneous combustion is not directly linked to pyrokinesis, there are some striking conclusions which have been logically discussed. One is that these people could be the victims of a person practicing pyrokinetics. Other people believe that it is possible these people were practicing exercises of pyrokinesis and were not able to control the fire completely. It is thought that with this inability to control the fire that they turned it upon themselves which resulted in them spontaneously combusting themselves.

Exercises to Develop your Pyrokinesis

When you train, you will be able to control fire. After a long time of practice, you will be able to extinguish and reignite a flame. You will only be able to hone this skill with continuous practice, unwavering concentration and meditation. Because pyrokinesis can be quite dangerous for beginners, you must be extremely careful when practicing as you will have no control of the fire at first. This is the reason why in many cases training for pyrokinesis should only be done after mastering telekinesis skills.

1. Light a candle is a space which there are no movements of the air.
2. Gaze at the flame and concentrate your focus solely on the fire.
3. Create a connection in your mind between you and the flame.

4. Close your eyes and envision the flame as vivid and detailed as possible. Feel the energy of the flame within yourself.
5. Open your eyes and gaze at the flame once more.
6. Visualize in your mind the flame moving to the right. Do not be upset if this does not occur after many days or months of practicing this feat.
7. Do not strain yourself and your energy to move the flame. You need to flow with the energy of the flame.
8. Once you have successfully moved the flame to the right, manipulate it by making it move to the left and also getting larger.
9. When you are able to manipulate the flame with your willpower, start to practice extinguishing the flame. Take a break if you are straining and stressing your energy.
10. With this same concentration, envision that the flame is extinguished. This will likely take more time than you mastering manipulating the direction of the flame, so do not get discouraged.
11. Once you are able to extinguish the fire with your mind, try to reignite the flame. It is more simple if

you are able to complete this quickly after the flame has been extinguished.

Another practice you can work with is known as the Dancing Flame.

1. Light a candle in a room with no air movement.
2. Gaze upon the flame as you visualize a tunnel between the flame and you.
3. Create a connection of the energy of the flame.
4. Once the energy is connected, imagine a sphere of white energy and send it towards the flame through the tunnel.
5. Now move the sphere in different directions around the candle – higher, lower or to the sides – to manipulate the flame.
6. After you are able to accomplish this manipulation of the flame, you can move forward to extinguishing the flame.
7. Place the white energy ball over the flame to remove the oxygen so that the flame will go out.
8. Remember to take breaks if you are stressing or straining your mind.

The Basics of Empathy

There are several steps that you can take to embrace and strengthen your personal empathic skills. Here there is going to be a comprehensive set of methods to learn more about different empathic skills, way to utilize them for the greatest benefit as well as ways to continue to build up these particular talents.

Every person has the capability of deepening their intuition and empathy levels where you are able to use these God given talents to help not only you, but more importantly the world as a whole. To do this, you must put on your battle face as you are going to be strengthening these attributes by having a strong spirit.

Self-care is the number one step in making sure that you are able to not only use these talents that you have been given, but to continue to work and grow with them. It is a hard process at times, but when has anything not worth having been handed to you on a platter? These methods will take hard work and dedication. You must keep your end goals in mind which will keep your spirit strong during the tough parts of the process so that you can enjoy the full benefits and be able to help others to the best of your ability.

Your self-care is something that comes before any one person or situation. How are you able to help others fully when you are only half energized and centered? These self-care practices will keep your being strong, centered and continue to thrive. When you implement self-care daily, you will become unstoppable as your energy will be reserved for times that you are needing it. It will not continue to be siphoned away by others who are wanting to feed off your energy. You will not take on emotions and feelings that you are not willing to take on. It makes you ever strong in the sensitive world of the empath.

The following are five methods which can be used on a daily basis to continue to build up your strong spirit so that you can then work on strengthening your other empathic skills:

Be Grateful and Express Gratefulness Whenever Possible

When you wake up, start your day on the correct foot by expressing gratitude. First off, there are many people who did not get the same privilege. At the very least, you should be grateful about you breathing, your health, and other blessings including family and being able to help others.

You can continue to find gratefulness in the difficult situations that you possess. These are the greatest things to be grateful for because they are in your life to teach you the most. When you can change your perspective on these "bad" things, it will lift you up even higher in your gratitude.

When you practice gratitude on a daily basis as part of your self-care, it makes you more self-aware, keeps you in the moment and builds positive energy. It also will keep you more energized as you will not be bleeding energy by imagining things that will happen in the future or wasting worry on things that have happened in the past.

You can also utilize this method throughout the day to continue building up the positive energy. Take the time to express your gratitude to the people who you come in contact with, your pets and your family members. You can extend this idea even to strangers who you can change their attitude with a simple smile. This also shows them appreciation in a subtle way. All of these little gestures add up and will continue to strengthen you throughout the day.

Love Yourself Fully

Recognize daily that you are unique individual that has a purpose in this world. You are a gift, and you are here to share and meld with the other gifts in this world. Consider coming up with a phrase or mantra which is special to you that will help you lift yourself up. If you are coming up with your own, try to incorporate all aspects of you in a short sentence which is powerful and impactful to your spirit and well being .

Other ways that you can love yourself is to listen to your body and adjust your day accordingly. Do not try to push yourself to the point where you are breaking when you are just waking up in the morning. Just like you need to stretch to warm up your body before exercise, you must allow yourself to wake up properly so that you are centered and focused on the tasks of the day.

Whatever makes you the happiest in your soul whether it is reading a certain book of inspiring quotes or drinking your favorite tea while watching the birds play out in your yard, take the time to nurture your spirit in the morning times, especially, even though this also can be applied throughout the day.

The properly love yourself, you must be quiet and listen to yourself so that you will know what your needs are. Once these needs are met, you will be able to be your full self to be able to share your healing energy with other people in a more impactful and helpful way.

Aware and Mindful Breathing

At some point during your morning routine, likely coupled with the meditation exercise, you need to empty your energy and spirit of any negativity and stress. This will not only help to calm your inner self, it will give you a sense of clarity and strengthen your energy throughout the day.

You are going to want to try to do this at the same time of the day and you can do this exercise at any time that you are feeling stress build up in your body. This will help you to keep your focus throughout the day as well. The morning exercise should be a minimum of ten minutes, but you can do whatever time length you feel comfortable as long as your stress and negativity is melted away.

The mindful breathing exercise is as follows:

1. Find a place in which you feel comfortable and shake the extremities of your body before you sit or lay down to help with the process of relaxation.

2. Breathe in deeply and long in through your nose while allowing your stomach to fill with air.

3. Hold the air for a few seconds.

4. Slowly let the air out through your mouth.

5. Do this practice for a minimum of three breaths before moving onto the next part of the exercise.

For the next section, you need to visualize a situation, place or phrase which brings you to a place of relaxation. Once you find this calm, continue on.

1. Close your eyes and continue to breath in through your nose.

2. As you are breathing, visualize the air you are breathing is full of calm and peace. Allow this feeling to immolate throughout your body.

3. Then breathe out slowly through your mouth while visualizing any tension or stress in your body leaving with the breath.

4. Continue to breathe in and out using the visualizations for the remainder of your breathing exercise time, for a minimum of ten minutes.

5. Continue on to the meditation practice if you wish for your daily self-care.

Exercises to Develop your Empathy

The Basics of Astral Projection

This is a skill that can be perfected which will allow you to have an out of body experience or a state of consciousness which is altered. It is experienced when your spirit is able to physically leave your body so that you can travel through different dimensions. Your spirit is not entirely detached from your body as there is a silver cord similar to an umbilical cord which keep the two connected. This cord is not able to be detached except through death, so there is no possibility of this cord breaking while your spirit is out of your body.

There is not simply one experience that you have when you astral project. Some people says that you can experience sensations of floating or flying in the sky while you are able to look down upon the world. You can also experience the world as if you were standing in the room, yet no one would be able to see and interact with you. Lucid dreaming is a type of astral projection since you are conscious of your activities during the sleep state.

Exercises to Develop your Astral Travel Skills

Like all of the other physic abilities, you need to use meditation to keep your mind focused and quiet. You will need to remove any doubts that you are able to accomplish and hone this skill, as these doubts will surely keep you from experiencing an out of body experience. You need to ensure that the space that you choose to astral project from is a comfortable temperature. It is also important to make sure that you are not going to get hungry, but do not eat a large meal ahead of time, otherwise you will likely go to sleep.

1. Sit or lay in a spot where you will not be disturbed. All the muscles in your body to relax.

2. Take deep and slow breaths in through your nose and out through your mouth.

3. Concentrate your focus on creating a white light which will cover your entire body.

4. Once you envision your body is covered in white light, imagine that it is floating up slowly.

5. As you see your body rising, your spirit and body will separate in your mind, leaving the physical

body where you first started. The spirit body is going to rise above the physical body.

6. Remove any fear or doubt in your mind. Choose a destination you would like to experience.

7. Once you have projected to another location and you want to return back, simply think of your physical body, and envision your spirit entering your physical body slowly.

Another method that you can use is known as The Rope

1. Envision yourself laying down with a rope laying on top of you.

2. Then imagine that you reach your hands out to the rope and start pulling yourself upwards.

3. Continue to pull upwards on the rope until you start to feel a vibration throughout your entire body.

4. As you continue to pull on the rope, you will start to feel the sensation of flying. This is when your spirit has separated from your physical body.

5. Let the rope go, and look downwards to see yourself lying down.

6. Return to your body by thinking of your spiritual body slowly entering your physical body once again.

One last technique was created by Muldoon, and it is known as his Thirst Technique. For this exercise, you need to refrain from drinking water throughout the entire day you want to practice. You will be using your want and need for water as an emotion which will drive you to bartering for an out of body experience.

1. Pour yourself a glass of water in a clear cup. Place it on a table in front of you.

2. Gaze at the glass of water as you imagine yourself drinking the water. Continue this practice for three hours.

3. Before you go to sleep, set the glass of water within a few feet of you and eat a pinch of salt. This will cause you to be craving water more.

4. As you lie in bed, continue to imagine yourself getting up out of bed and drinking the glass of water.

5. You will know this exercise is successful if you are able to astral project and drink the water in your spirit form.

The Risks and Benefits of Psychic Skills

There are some perks to being tapped and connected with your psychic skills. Once you start to delve deeper within this connection, you will realize that these benefits will touch on all areas of your life and bond you closer to yourself, your environment and those close to you.

It is important to note that these skills also come with their own responsibilities because if you use them for your personal benefit of an ill intention, they can quickly start to cause havoc in your life as well as others. An example of this would be someone who is able to see future events. Remember that the future is not static and is based upon possibilities. Refrain from telling people that something is sure to happen because their personal choices may change the outcome of your vision for their future.

You will start to see the world from a unique and different perspective. You will also have more clear insight into how to make decisions which will be for your greatest benefit and choosing the correct path for you. You will also feel more tapped in and find there is a natural flow of energy that takes you through life. You will be able to feel more at peace knowing that you have nothing truly to worry about because it is all part of a larger plan.

When you tap into these psychic energies, you need to be aware that they can come at a cost. They are meant to connect you to something much greater outside of yourself, but it must be respected. If you are wanting to strengthen these skills just to get personal gain, you are likely going to see a ripple effect of terrible things infiltrating your life and those surrounding you. Let me go over the main difficulties that you may face when you are learning about your skills and if you should use them for the wrong purpose.

There is a limit to the storage space of the energy within your system. While you are cultivating your skills, these energy levels will rise. Your body is able to adapt to these fluctuations in energy, and your space is going to grow over time. However, if you try to take on too many energies before your body adapts, it will result in overload of your system. You will simply will not be able to handle above and beyond the space that you body has dedicated to handling these energies.

The symptoms when you take on too much energy will be dizziness and headaches. You may feel like you have ADHD because you will lack the ability to focus, resulting in you loose your psychic skills temporarily. You may feel lost as you are swimming through the heightened amount of energy flowing through your body. If this should occur, consciously bring yourself down by grounding and centering yourself so that your energy will naturally neutralize. Take some time to nurture yourself by taking some alone time to revitalize your body.

In this same effect, you may be in the position where you are taking on too much information as you are developing your psychic skills. As you delve deeper into the process, you may come across information which may be an epiphany which your mind is not able to fully handle or comprehend at the moment. It may completely negative a firmly held belief you have had your entire life.

This is usually the case if you are working to build your psychic skills each day as a beginner. Be sure to listen to your body and your mind as you are going through this process. Do not push yourself if you should be feeling tired or hungry. If you are feel particularly stressed, take care of your physical self before you venture into your spiritual side.

If you are gifted with the vision of spirits, this may be an interesting and wanted experience, when it happens occasionally. However, the more that some people deepen their connection to the other side, they are able to see spirits all of the time as they mingle with living people. It may get to the point where you are not able to determine if they are spirits or living people, which can pose a problem.

If this should happen, be sure to talk to your other psychic friends to get support. They may also have some very good advice as to how to handle this. Grounding yourself on a daily basis will help this from occurring. Meditation is also very helpful to help continue to calm and focus your mind.

As you strengthen your intuitive and empathic skills, you may find that you are able to experience other people's pain and emotions. This can drive a person a bit mad if they are unaware that this wide range of symptoms and emotions that they are feeling are not actually their own. When you have other people's emotions mixed with your own, they can be conflicting, which makes you feel confused within yourself.

If you find that you are empathic in this way, make sure that you learn how to shield your energy from other people so that they are not able to meld with your own. Essentially you are building a protective bubble which cannot be penetrated. This will also help you in the case that other people are trying to drain you of your own energy.

Chapter 4 - Root Chakra Reiki Meditation for Day One Through Three

Overview of the Mooladhara Chakra - Root or 1st Chakra

Associated with the earth element, the purpose of this chakra is to give a firm foundation, support, stability and safety. It is associated with the sciatic nerve, bones, legs, feet. It is the location of the energy of existence. It connects our energy to the material world as well as primal survival. The color which is connected with the root chakra is red.

When this chakra is clear and balanced, you will feel happy to be alive as well as worthy of your existence. However, when this chakra is in need of work because of it being blocked, our perspective changes. We feel entitled to occupy our space or we may feel a lack of love or value. This negative thinking leads us to resent our existence as well as compare ourselves with others.

As you work on balancing the mooladhara chakra, you will start to trust in the flow of prosperity in all forms in your life. You will also strengthen your overall wellbeing and health along with your sense of security. Exercises based on opening and charging the 1st chakra contains the pranic energy. It also is the place in which our hidden or darker sides of our nature are concealed, sometimes even from ourselves.

Responsibilities of the Root Chakra

It is extremely important to pay special attention to the 1st chakra because making sure that it is healed, cleared, opened and balanced is key for the other chakras to do the same. This is the energy center where all of your basic needs are addressed. The term *Muladhara* translates into *base* or *root support*. The main influences of the root chakra are the following:

- ❖ You confidence levels
- ❖ Your survival
- ❖ Your sense of security and safety
- ❖ Your drive for basic physical needs like rest, shelter and food
- ❖ Your feeling of being grounded

Imbalance Symptoms

A root chakra imbalance can easily throw your entire system out of order. When your base chakra is in alignment, you will feel an overall peace while also feeling comfortable with your life, relaxed and stable. However, when this chakra is misaligned or blocked, you will feel quite insecure as well as worried about your basic needs. It will also raise your anxiety and stress levels as you continue to worry. You may also have problems with one or a combination of the following:

- ❖ Feeling overwhelmed easily by bright lights, loud noises or crowds
  Major illness plague you such as depression,fibromyalgia, fatigue and chronic pain
- ❖ Overly care for people who are physically and mentally able.
- ❖ Heightened feeling of panic or being threatened which can lead to racing heart, hyperventilation and panic attacks.
- ❖ Overall feeling of uncertainty
- ❖ Lack of concentration due to preoccupation with worry.
- ❖ Cold extremities

- ❖ Low energy levels
- ❖ Sore lower back
- ❖ Pain in the legs
- ❖ Digestive upset
- ❖ Negativity towards yourself and other people
- ❖ An unhealthy relationship with food such as purging, binging or starving.
- ❖ Low self-confidence levels
- ❖ Extreme reliance on external feedback for validation

These imbalances and blockages can happen due to a singular event such as a conflict with a friend of family member, financial difficulties or losing a job suddenly.

Day 1 Root Chakra Physical Meditation

It is important to have your chakras straightened and centered before performing grounding and meditation practices. This ensures that your energy is flowing properly throughout your body and will bring the best benefit to your grounding and meditation exercises. **Be**

sure to perform this each day before you start your meditation practice.

To center yourself, you will simply:

1. Stand up straight with your hands down by your side. You can stand against a wall to ensure your body is straight. Alternatively, you can do this exercise while sitting down with your feet flat on the floor.

2. Visualize a line going from the top of your head down through your back straight down to the ground.

You can now move onto the practice of grounding. It is a simple practice that can be done practically anywhere. It is best to do this outside where you are able to place your bare feet on the ground. However, the same principle can occur anywhere, even with shoes on. The point of this exercise is to make you feel more connected with the earth as well as being fully present in the moment within your body.

To ground yourself:

1. Stand outside on the dirt, grass or sit in a chair with your feet firmly planted on the ground.

2. Breathe deep through your mouth. As you are breathing in, visualize white light encompassing your body.

3. As you breathe out through your nose, direct the breath visually down   through your feet.

4. Continue with this cycle of breathing until the sense of calmness overtakes you again which usually takes a minimum of three breaths.

The follow through to the physical root chakra meditation:

1. While starting this mediation, breathe with intent while focusing your attention to the base of your spine, the location of the root chakra.

2. While standing in a comfortable position, make fists out of your hands and   hold them tight for two to three seconds.

3. Continue to clench your fists for five rounds.

4. Shake your hands to release the energy and allow them to become relaxed.

5. Then rub your hands together for several seconds until you feel them become warm and electrified.

6. Clap your hands together forcefully once the point has been reached that your hands are full of electric   pulses.

7. Put one foot out in front of you while pointing your toes. Hold for a couple of seconds.

8. Move your foot up and down vertically to stretch out your ankles while   holding in both positions for a couple of seconds.

9. Repeat the last two steps with your other foot.

10. Set your hands on your knees and quickly rub your thighs up towards your hips and then back to your knees.

11. Repeat this step a few times or until heat is generated in your thighs.

12. Now stand straight with your hands resting by your side.

13. Raise one hand above your head as high as you can as you breath in through your nose.

14. Then lower your hand slowly as you breath out through your mouth.

15. Repeat with your other hand and practice this for a few   rounds.

16. Once complete, leave your arms loosely at your sides as you rest for a   moment.

17. During this rest period, intently pay attention to your energy levels in the root chakra as you mindfully breathe in and out.

18. Continue to release any negativity and stress in your 1st chakra with each breath out. Breathe in

healing and positive energy.

19. Now take a walk in the park or in nature for a period that you set so that you can recharge and balance your first chakra.

Day 2 Root Chakra Mental Meditation

1. Sit on the floor in a cross legged or kneeling position. Alternatively you can sit in a chair with your feet flat on the floor.
2. Keep your shoulders, back and your spine straight.
3. Relax all your muscles, closing your eyes and take a few normal breaths.
4. Inhale deeply and fully through the nose. Pull the breath as far down into your body as you can. Exhale slowly through the mouth. Repeat for 3 breaths.
5. Then turn your focus to the area of the root chakra. Take note of any tightness in the area.
6. Envision a ball of red energy at your root chakra. Manipulate this ball in your mind so that it expands. Then start to see it spin.

7. As the red ball of energy grows, feel the sensation of your root chakra as it becomes relaxed and warm.

8. Once your 1st chakra feels warm, continue to meditate while feeling this sensation of warmth between five and ten minutes.

9. With every breathe in, see and believe that you are breathing in positive and healing energy. While you breathe out, envision you release the negative, stagnant and stale energy.

10. When you have completed, slowly open your eyes.

11. Rest in this space for a few minutes before trying to get up.

Day 3 Root Chakra Spiritual Meditation

Each chakra has what is known as a beej mantra which is a word from Sanskrit. Chanting these mantras create a specific sound and vibration which resonates with each chakra in a unique way, helping to clear and balance your energy centers as well as connecting you to the higher power outside of yourself.

1. Sit comfortably in a meditation posture which is comfortable for you. This can be on a yoga mat, cushion or a chair.
2. Close your eyes and take in three normal breaths, focusing on the flow of the air throughout your body.
3. Concentrate upon your root chakra as you envision red throughout your sight of vision.
4. Take note how the color makes you feel.
5. Place the tip of your tongue on the back section of the upper palate on the roof of your mouth.
6. Focus the red into a sphere at the base of your spine.
7. As you breathe in, focus your concentration on the sphere.
8. Chant the sound "loom" for each slow release of breath as you envision the red sphere vibrating.
9. With each breathe, see the sphere getting larger and more vibrant.
10. Continue chanting between three and five minutes as you continue to concentrate on the root chakra sensations.
11. As you breathe in, fill yourself with positive energies. Allow the breath as it exits your body to

take away any of the blockages and tension that you feel.

12. When the exercise is complete, slowly open your eyes and take your time moving when you are comfortable to do so.

Chapter 5 - Sacral Chakra Reiki Meditation Day Four Through Six

Overview of the Svadhisthana Chakra - Sacral or 2nd Chakra

The sacral chakra is associated with the element of water. The purpose is to allow pleasure, emotional wellbeing, expansion, flow and movement. The areas of the body which are connected with this chakra are the joints, inner thighs, sex organs, lower abdomen, sacrum and hips. The color of orange is associated with the sacral chakra. It is also responsible for helping us to trust our sensation. As we are drawn to the things that make us feel good, this chakra is starting to open up. When we trust our instincts, we are able to surrender to our highest consciousness and allow nature to work her creative force through us.

When this chakra is blocked, which means the pranic energy is not able to freely flow, we no longer have the trust as we have lost the connection to our intuition and source of our feelings. As we are separated from our higher power, we start to feel negativity, lethargy and depression. If you are a person who must be in control of their lives, it is usually because the 2nd chakra is out of balance as you feel as if everything is out of control. The truth is, you must accept that much of everything is out of your control. Only when this thought of control is surrendered will you feel more at peace.

Responsibilities of the Sacral Chakra

The 2nd chakra is related to anything to do with creation and creativity. It also has an association to personal growth, imagination and sex drive. It is located in the middle of the abdomen about two inches below the belly button. It influences your feeling of:

- ❖ Feedback of artistic pursuits
- ❖ Your confidence level in what you create
- ❖ Pleasure you feel in life
- ❖ Satisfaction in romantic relationship
- ❖ Ability to be playful with others
- ❖ Inspiration level you experience

Imbalance Symptoms

When this chakra is open, you have an overall feeling of being stimulated as well being full of ideas. You will also feel heightened confidence to proceed with significant changes in your lifestyle. However, when this chakra is out of balance, your life will feel stifling, repetitive and boring. Your sacral chakra can become quickly closed if you have any negative feedback about sexuality or creativity. Other common symptoms are:

* Losing sleep while worrying too much or heightened anxiety level
* Suffer from passive aggressiveness and resentfulness when others only take from them
* Isolating themselves from other people and normal activities
* Becoming addicted to substances such as alcohol, medications or illegal drugs
* Lack of creativity
* Cyclical dysfunctional relationships
* Lack of motivation
* Diminished sexual appetite or unpleasant sexual intercourse

- ❖ Emotional confusion
- ❖ You feel unimportant and thinks that no one loves you
- ❖ You cannot take care of yourself or you feel you do not know how
- ❖ You tend to hang your shoulders bent forward
- ❖ Easily offended
- ❖ Fear of change
- ❖ Massive amounts of guilt about the past
- ❖ Low self-worth
- ❖ Frequent bouts of jealousy
- ❖ Heightened issues with allergy symptoms
- ❖ Bladder discomfort
- ❖ Low energy
- ❖ Gambling, shopping addiction and eating issues

Some common causes of these symptoms are based on associations with sexuality, creativity and change. You may find that you have sexual incompatibility in a relationship, rejection of your creative words, reproductive issues or rejection from a crush or love.

This chakra is associated with water which means that any activities in body of water will help balance the energy. If you are not around any sources of water, a long and soothing bath will do the trick as well. When you eat foods which are orange such as mangoes, melons, oranges or carrots, you will clear this chakra.

Day 4 Sacral Chakra Physical Meditation

To enhance this meditation, you can perform it by a body of water such as a lake, river or ocean. If these are not available and you would like to incorporate this idea into your meditation, you can also draw a bath.

1. Sit comfortably in a meditation posture which is comfortable for you. This can be on a yoga mat, cushion or a chair.
2. Close your eyes and take in three normal breaths, inhaling through your nose and breathing out through your mouth.
3. Envision a stream of light shining down on the top of your head and having the light flow through your body all the way to your toes.
4. This light is going to wash away any tension that is present in your body as you allow your muscles to loosen and relax.

5. Now imagine that light slowing moving up your legs up to your waist. Pause it there for a short time, as you feel comfortable.

6. Then push this light up to your chest and covering your shoulders and back.

7. Allow this light to flow down your arms to the tips of your fingers.

8. Push this light up your neck, throat, face up to the top of your head.

9. Sit while focusing on your breathing as well as the sensations that are felt throughout your body for a minimum of 10 minutes.

10. When you are ready, slowly open your eyes and take note of your quality of your mind afterwards. Make an intention to keep your mind in this space throughout the day.

Day 5 Sacral Chakra Mental Meditation

1. Sit in a comfortable and quiet place. Keep your back and neck straight with your limbs relaxed.

2. Take ten slow, deep breaths in through your nose and out through your mouth.

3. Envision a spinning orange sphere at your sacral chakra.

4. Imagine the orange light rippling outwards until it covers your entire body.

5. Feel the sensation that your body is warming up.

6. Continue to focus on your breath and keep feeling this orange energy for a minimum of five minutes.

7. When you are ready, slowly open your eyes and take your time getting back up on your feet.

8. Do this for as long as you like (preferably for at least five minutes), then open your eyes when you're ready.

Day 6 Sacral Chakra Spiritual Meditation

1. Sit comfortably in a meditation posture which is comfortable for you. This can be on a yoga mat, cushion or a chair.

2. Close your eyes and take in three normal breaths, focusing on the flow of the air throughout your body.

3. Concentrate upon your sacral chakra as you envision orange throughout your sight of vision.

4. Take note how the color makes you feel as your body starts to warm up.

5. Place your upper set of teeth on the inner section of your lower lip.

6. In this position, you will sound similar to a car revving up when you breath out.

7. Focus on the orange sphere, as you breathe in. Focus your concentration on the sphere.

8. Chant the sound "vahm" for each slow release of breath as you envision the red sphere vibrating.

9. With each breathe, see the sphere getting larger and more vibrant.

10. Continue chanting between three and five minutes as you continue to concentrate on the 2nd chakra sensations.

11. As you breathe in, fill yourself with positive energies. Allow the breath as it exits your body to take away any of the blockages and tension that you feel.

12. When the exercise is complete, slowly open your eyes and take your time moving when you are comfortable to do so.

Chapter 6 - Solar Plexus Chakra Reiki Meditation Day Seven Through Nine

Overview of the Manipura Chakra - Solar Plexus or 3rd Chakra

This chakra is associated with fire and has the purpose of change, transformation, willpower, strength and energy. The ribs, adrenal glands, digestive organs and upper abdomen are associated with the 3rd chakra. When there are any issues with these parts of the body, this chakra is in need of attention and energetic cleansing. The navel was where everyone was once connected to their mothers through the umbilical cord. Of course we relied in this cord for our connection and nutrients from our mother. Even after the umbilical cord is cut, this connection will always be present in the navel.

On an energetic level, this chakra holds the power and consciousness of our spiritual selves. As the prana flows through our manipura chakra, is gives the sustained energy the same as the sunshine. This is why the color yellow is associated with this chakra. It also gives us the capability of manifesting with confidence on this plane.

In the case of Kundalini awakening, the 3rd chakra is where the true awakening happens as this is the location where the internal fire is ignited and sent through to the other chakras. It is also the seat of our gut instinct as we feel if something is off in this chakra. These messages are extremely important to listen to as this is the connection to our internal guidance system.

If this chakra is out of balance, you will feel uncertain about your choices as well as your day-to-day decisions. As you work on opening and clearing the navel chakra, you will feel a sense of balance and you will be more sensitive to the messages from your gut instinct. Once you start to practice listening, you will be able to feel as if you are in the correct flow with the universe.

Responsibilities of the Solar Plexus

The 3rd chakra is in direct alignment with your ability to cultivate your skill and make the best decisions because you will be able to see the bigger picture of a situation. You will also experience heightened confidence and self-esteem levels. It is located in the stomach area at the top of your abdomen and is commonly known as the personal power chakra. The solar plexus is responsible for the following:

- ❖ How you define your purpose
- ❖ Your level of independence
- ❖ If you learn lessons from difficult situations
- ❖ Self-discipline levels
- ❖ Your ability for self-forgiveness
- ❖ Whether you envision yourself as being good enough
- ❖ Your response to criticism from others.

Imbalance Symptoms

With the 3rd chakra in balance you will be certain of the steps needed to succeed, you are sure of your identity and are self-assured. When this chakra is out of balance, you will find that you will have difficulty with sudden changes or moving from your past mistakes. You are also able to have an oversensitive chakra when out of alignment which may lead to anxiety issues or mania. Symptoms you may experience when the solar plexus is not open are:

- ❖ Not exercising personal boundaries or standing up for themselves
- ❖ Attracting energy vampires and negative people
- ❖ Cannot let things go and soak up toxic and negative energy
- ❖ Low self-esteem levels
- ❖ Lack of direction or purpose
- ❖ Feeling helpless
- ❖ Feeling the need to control everyone and everything around you
- ❖ Feelings of worthlessness
- ❖ Nausea
- ❖ Bloating
- ❖ Short-term memory issues
- ❖ Digestive cramps

The element for this chakra is fire. Create a bonfire and sit around it while basking in the fire. Alternatively, sit in the bright afternoon sunshine for at least twenty minutes. Changes in the diet should include yellow foods such as corn, pineapple, turmeric, ginger and bananas.

The element for this chakra is fire. Create a bonfire and sit around it while basking in the fire. Alternatively, sit in the bright afternoon sunshine for at least twenty minutes. Changes in the diet should include yellow foods such as corn, pineapple, turmeric, ginger and bananas.

Day 7 Solar Plexus Chakra Physical Meditation

1. Sit in a comfortable position and take note about your mental and physical state.
2. Take a few deep breaths while inhaling through your nose and exhaling through your mouth.
3. As you exhale, release the tension and pressure within your body and mind.
4. If there are any tense areas of your body, focus you attention by relaxing them on each exhale.
5. Envision a place in your mind where you are completely calm and at ease.
6. Be detailed about your picture of your happy place with all of the smells, sounds and sights you can experience.
7. Continue to breathe slowly and deeply as you continue to envision and enjoy this space you have created for a minimum of five minutes.

8. Create a space where all of your dreams and aspirations are true for you. Take note of how this space makes you feel as you build yourself higher.

9. When you are ready, slowly open your eyes and reflect on your feelings towards yourself.

10. Take your time getting back up on your feet.

Day 8 Solar Plexus Chakra Mental Meditation

1. Sit in a comfortable spot where you will not be disturbed.

2. Take in a few deep and long breaths in through your nose and out through your mouth as you clear your mind.

3. Focus your attention on your solar plexus chakra.

4. Envision a sphere of yellow at the center of your chakra. Take the time to grow the sphere in size and intensity.

5. Manipulate the sphere to spin as it is growing. You will find that your body is going to grow warm during this process.

6. Sit in this space while controlling your breath between three to five minutes.

7. Take notice of how the energy makes your body feel inside and out.

8. When you are ready to open your eyes, take three additional deep breaths before doing so.

Day 9 Solar Plexus Chakra Spiritual Meditation

1. Sit comfortably in a meditation posture which is comfortable for you. This can be on a yoga mat, cushion or a chair.

2. Close your eyes and take in three normal breaths, focusing on the flow of the air throughout your body.

3. Concentrate your attention of the lower middle section of your back. Envision yellow throughout your sight of vision.

4. Take note how the color makes you feel.

5. Place the tip of your tongue on the front section of the upper palate near your teeth on the roof of your mouth.

6. Focus the yellow into a sphere at the spine where you have focused concentration.

7. As you breathe in, focus your concentration on the sphere.

8. Chant the sound "rrahm" by rolling the "r"for each slow release of breath as you envision the yellow sphere vibrating.

9. With each breathe, see the sphere getting larger and more vibrant.

10. Continue chanting between three and five minutes as you continue to concentrate on the root chakra sensations.

11. As you breathe in, fill yourself with positive energies. Allow the breath as it exits your body to take away any of the blockages and tension that you feel.

12. When the exercise is complete, slowly open your eyes and take your time moving when you are comfortable to do so.

Chapter 7 - Heart Chakra Reiki Meditation Day Ten Through Twelve

Overview of the Anahata Chakra - Heart or 4th Chakra

The air is associated with the heart chakra. It is commonly known to have the purpose of union, connection, relationships, expansion and love. The parts of the body that are associated with the 4th chakra are the shoulder blades, respiratory system, heart, ribs, diaphragm, lungs and chest. This is an important chakra to have cleared and energized as it helps you to relate to others outside of yourself.

The color which is connected with this chakra is green and it is the most powerful chakra center in the human body. When Kundalini energy is released from the navel to the heart chakra, it brings a cascade of spiritual, emotional and physiological changes. We are able to resonate with the truth of our feelings when this occurs as the heart has the capability of transcending everything.

When we are doing anything based in emotions, they are based in the heart chakra. It could be a memory, vulnerability or even when we are speaking to others in a heartfelt way. It is through the 4th chakra that we are able to inspire other people. When this chakra has been activated, it is not solely depending on outside sources. In fact, internally you need to experience empathy which is self-sustaining and deep to fully connect with yourself and others.

When the anahata chakra is out of balance, you do not pay attention and ignore your own needs. You may also start to cling to others and become codependent for the support that you require rather than giving that support to yourself. Of course when you start to clear and charge this chakra, you will become more compassionate and giving to yourself and others.

The heart chakra is positioned directly above the heart. So, slightly to the left at the center of your chest. Sometimes called the Anahata, it both responds to and helps to shape your capacity for compassion, affection, and love.

Responsibilities of the Heart Chakra

The 4th chakra is located in the middle of your chest next to your chest. It is a type of bridge between your spirituality, emotions and thought. You heart chakra has a connection with:

- ❖ How much peace you feel
- ❖ Your capacity to self-reflect
- ❖ Knowledge of self
- ❖ Emotional openness
- ❖ Intensity that you are able to care about others
- ❖ Your level of empathy

Imbalance Symptoms

When your heart chakra is balanced, you are a giving and compassionate person who is also calm and loving. This is directed towards yourself and others, and you keep boundaries well for your own well-being. When it is not open, you are going to feel emotionally hurt for anything that does not happen your way. It can also quickly drain your emotional resources. Other symptoms include:

- ❖ Putting other people's needs first and showing codependent tendencies
- ❖ Staying in an abusive or negative relationship
- ❖ Attract bullies and narcissist personalities lack of empathy
- ❖ Irritability or impatience
- ❖ Difficulty in trusting other people
- ❖ Restlessness
- ❖ A decrease in the effectiveness of the immune system
- ❖ Raised or high blood pressure
- ❖ Insomnia
- ❖ Struggle to relate to others

Toxic and difficult romantic and non-romantic relationships can quickly close off the heart chakra. You might be dealing with an intense amount of emotions that you do not know how to deal with, loss or grief, cutting ties with someone or a lover who does not reciprocate. You can also be having a hard time accepting a specific truth about yourself.

The air is associated with the heart chakra. Deep breathing exercises will eliminate the blocked energy. You could also take a boat ride, fly a kite or open the windows of your home, office or car. Green foods will clear this chakra. Examples include spinach, kale, avocado and broccoli.

Day 10 Heart Chakra Physical Meditation

1. Sit on a cushion or a chair with your feet flat on the ground. Relax your muscles as you take a few deep and long breaths. Breathe in through your nose and out through your mouth smoothly.
2. Close your eyes slowly and envision a flame within your heart chakra as you continue with your smooth and long breaths.
3. Keep the flame burning steady. You will notice that any distractions to your thoughts or otherwise is going to cause the flame to flicker and waver.
4. Keep this meditation and concentration on keeping the flame constant for a minimum of ten minutes, but no more than half an hour.
5. When are ready, slowly open your eyes and continue to breathe steadily until you are ready to stand up.

Day 11 Heart Chakra Mental Meditation

1. Sit in a comfortable, relaxing place where you will not be disturbed.

2. Breathe in through your nose and out through your mouth for three minutes. Continue to relax your muscles as you breathe.

3. Envision green energy flowing up through your body towards the heart starting at the 1st chakra.

4. Picture the green energy creating a sphere at your heart chakra. As you inhale and exhale, see that ball becoming larger and more vibrant.

5. Focus on tuning into feelings of love for yourself and others as you allow the green energy to permeate your whole body.

6. Continue this meditation between three and five minutes.

7. Carefully open your eyes slowly and take your time getting back to your feet.

Day 12 Heart Chakra Spiritual Meditation

1. Sit comfortably in a meditation posture which is comfortable for you. This can be on a yoga mat, cushion or a chair.

2. Close your eyes and take in three normal breaths, focusing on the flow of the air throughout your body.

3. Concentrate upon your heart chakra as you envision green throughout your sight of vision.

4. Take note how the color makes you feel.

5. Focus the green into a sphere on your spine behind your heart chakra.

6. As you breathe in through your mouth, chant the sound "yum" as the air fills your mouth and throat.

7. With each breathe, see the sphere getting larger and more vibrant.

8. Continue chanting for a minimum of 10 minutes up to half an hour as you continue to concentrate on the heart chakra sensations.

9. As you breathe in, fill yourself with positive energies. Allow the breath as it exits your body to take away any of the blockages and tension that you feel.

10. When the exercise is complete, slowly open your eyes and take your time moving when you are comfortable to do so.

Chapter 8 - Throat Chakra Reiki Meditation Day Thirteen Through Fifteen

Overview of the Vishuddha Chakra - Throat or 5th Chakra

The element of sound is associated with the throat chakra where refinement, purification and communication is the purpose. The body parts which are associated with the 5th chakra are the ears, mouth, tongue, throat, neck and shoulders. If there is any sort of imbalance with these areas of your body, you are in need of clearing and charging of the vishuddha chakra.

Because the 5th chakra corresponds to the throat, it is the energy center in which we are able to speak with our authentic voice. It is where choices turn into actions and allows us to make focused choice on how we want to communicate with others. The color which is used with this chakra is blue. It is where our true self originate as we express who we are with the outside world.

When you realize that this chakra is not receiving pranic energy, you will have expressing emotions or true thoughts. You will put out a kind face to the world and try to be polite at all times when in truth it is not resonating with how you feel in your heart. This is a form of denying your truth which is what causes the blockages in this chakra. When you start to work on opening the throat chakra, you will be able to express your true feelings and thoughts without fear in a loving way.

If everything in your life is going well, all of these chakras will be aligned and in harmony. You'll be happy, healthy and at peace. In contrast, a blockage in one or more of the chakras can make you feel profoundly unsettled.

Responsibilities of the Throat Chakra

The throat chakra is located in the middle of your throat and is connected to your communication and self-expression skills. It will have an impact on:

* ❖ Awareness of your needs
* ❖ Your capability to be heard

- ❖ The quality of your relationships
- ❖ How you react to confrontation or conflict
- ❖ If you live your life authentically
- ❖ Your emotional honesty

- ❖

Imbalance Symptoms

When this 5th chakra is open, you will be able to communicate clearly and be able to express any of your views with tact. You will have an understanding of what you need and be able to put your words across in ways that people will want to listen. When the throat chakra is out of balance, you will find that you feel that people do not listen to you and you will have difficulty communicating with others.

- ❖ Unable to stop listening to someone who is venting or spouting off with negativity Listening to people's problems even when it is inconvenient
- ❖ Feeling like people do not know the real you
- ❖ Feel like you have many secrets
- ❖ Lacking the words to describe your emotions

- ❖ An achy or stiff neck
- ❖ Drastic changes in hormone levels
- ❖ Sore throat

If you are having problems with the throat chakra closing, try not to be so hard on yourself. You may have past experiences where it was painful to communicate such as a harsh argument that has stuck with you. You could also have difficulty with opening this chakra is you were told as a child to keep your feelings to yourself.

Ether is the element for the throat chakra. Sitting in a space where you can enjoy the clear sky will remove the blocked energy. Alternatively, eat blue foods such as dragon fruit, currants and blueberries.

Day 13 Throat Chakra Physical Meditation

1. Sit in a comfortable position on a yoga mat, cushion or chair. Place your feet flat on the floor if you are sitting in a chair.
2. Close your eyes and breathe in three smooth and deep breaths in through your nose and out through your mouth.

3. Focus your concentration on your breathing and the flow throughout your body.

4. As you exhale, pay special attention to the sound of the breath entering and exiting your body.

5. Continue your focus on your breath between three to five minutes, noting the sensations of the air in the throat.

6. When you have completed your allotted time, slowly open your eyes and get up slowly to your feet.

Day 14 Throat Chakra Mental Meditation

1. Sit down in a comfortable chair with a straight back in a place you will not be disturbed.

2. Inhale and exhale ten times smooth and deep. Breathe in through your nose and exhale through your mouth.

3. Starting at the top of your head, mentally scan down the body and imagine your muscles relaxing as pass your body over.

4. When your muscles are relaxed, envision a spinning, vibrant blue ball at your throat chakra.

5. Imagine the sphere is growing larger and brighter.

6. As it grows, imagine your throat chakra expanding and clearing at the same time.

7. Allow the blue energy to take over the energy of all your body.

8. Sit with this energy, continuing to focus on your breath between three and five minutes.

9. When you are done, slowly open your eyes and take your time getting back to your feet.

Day 15 Throat Chakra Spiritual Meditation

1. Sit comfortably in a meditation posture which is comfortable for you. This can be on a yoga mat, cushion or a chair.

2. Close your eyes and take in three normal breaths, focusing on the flow of the air throughout your body.

3. Concentrate upon the spine at your neck as you envision blue throughout your sight of vision.

4. Take note how the color makes you feel.

5. Focus the blue into a sphere at your throat chakra at the spine.

6. As you breathe in, focus your concentration on the sphere as you say "hum" pronounced like humming.

7. Release the breath as you envision the blue sphere vibrating as the air passes through your throat.

8. With each breathe, see the sphere getting larger and more vibrant.

9. Continue chanting between three and five minutes as you continue to concentrate on the throat chakra vibrations.

10. As you breathe in, fill yourself with positive energies. Allow the breath as it exits your body to take away any of the blockages and tension that you feel.

11. When the exercise is complete, slowly open your eyes and take your time moving when you are comfortable to do so.

Chapter 9 - The Third Eye Reiki Meditation Day Sixteen Through Eighteen

Overview of the Ajna Chakra - Third Eye or 6th Chakra

The 6th chakra is associated with the element of light and gives the person imagination, vision, wisdom, guidance and insight when it is clear and charged. The pineal gland, forehead and eyes are associated with the third eye chakra. It is where our sixth sense and intuition reside and is associated with the color of indigo.

The ajna chakra is the seat of the hormones for wakefulness and sleep are released as the area between your eyebrows is sensitive to the light of day and the absence of light in the darkness. When you continue to work with the 6th chakra, you will become more empathic and sensitive towards the feelings of others and also the universe.

Continued work to clear and charge this chakra will also the Kundalini Shakti to open and close your third eye to give you insight into situations as needed. When it is balanced, you will know all the answers that you need to know when you need to know them. There is no need to search outwardly for answers. You will simply know intuitively as you will trust your higher consciousness fully. However, if this chakra is not balanced, you will have a difficult time of making decisions which are clear and to your highest benefit.

Ranging from the root chakra at the bottom of the spine to the crown chakra at the top of the head, all seven chakras are powerful energy centers.

The aim is to use chakra exercises to keep all these energy centers open and balanced. If you can achieve this, you'll be better able to fulfill your full potential and live a happy life. In contrast, the more chakras are blocked or misaligned, the more you'll sense something is wrong.

Responsibilities of the Third Eye Chakra

Your third eye chakra is situated between your eyebrows and is your direct connection to your spirituality. It has an affect on the following:

- ❖ Your feeling of being stuck, stagnant or moving forward
- ❖ Your balance between reason and emotion
- ❖ Your ability to see the bigger picture of life

- ❖ Your capability to form accurate gut feelings

Imbalance Symptoms

With your 6th chakra in balance, you will be able to make big decisions based on a balance of logic and emotions. You will have a solid trust in your intuition and know that you are living your purpose in life. Because you trust your intuition, you will naturally flow towards opportunities which are right for you and to your highest purpose. You will also be more mindful about yourself and the world around you. When the third eye is closed, you will doubt your intuition or the existence of it which will make you question everything. Other common symptoms include:

- ❖ Feel as if the weight of the world is on their shoulders alone and feel responsible
- ❖ Mood swings due to taking on other people's moods
- ❖ Paranoia
- ❖ Believing that your life or career is insignificant
- ❖ General indecisiveness
- ❖ Lack of faith within yourself or your purpose
- ❖ Sinus pain
- ❖ Leg and back pain
- ❖ Eye discomfort
- ❖ Migraines or headaches
- ❖ Trouble sleeping or insomnia
- ❖ Struggle to learn new concepts
- ❖ Clumsy
- ❖ Cynicism
- ❖ Overly logical or emotional
- ❖ Often lost in your thoughts
- ❖ Frequently escape into daydreaming to avoid reality

- ❖ Addicted to external things such as shopping, status, money, sex, food or relationships which you believe will bring you happiness
- ❖ Interactions with other people are very trivial or superficial
- ❖ Mistrust or dislike people easily
- ❖ Stubbornness
- ❖ Suffer from delusions or mental illness

You may find that your chakra becomes closed after someone belittles your passion or career. Also instances of transitions in life such as divorce, job loss, death or illness will cause a misalignment.

This chakra is coupled with light. To heal this chakra, sit in a sunny window or in the direct sunlight. Indigo foods such as blackberries, grapes and purple kale will help as well.

Day 16 Third Eye Chakra Physical Meditation

1. Go outside in a place you will not be disturbed where you are able to see the moon clearly.
2. Sit down in a comfortable position and take a few deep and long breaths. Breathe in through the nose and out through your mouth.
3. Relax the muscles in your body and sink into the earth.
4. Gaze upon the moon for as long as possible without blinking your eyes. As you gaze, envision the moon as an experience occurring within you.
5. Become one with the energy of the moon as you feel it reverberating within you.
6. Once this occurs, close your eyes slowly and focus your eyes upwards to the third eye. You should still see an image of the moon. If not, take in 5 long and deep breaths and focus on the movement of air in your body.
7. When the image of the moon disappears from your mind's eye, open your eyes once again to gaze upon the moon.

8. This is one round. Keep repeating as many times as necessary to practice this exercise for a minimum of 15 minutes until you are feeling too much strain in your eyes.

Day 17 Third Eye Chakra Mental Meditation

1. Sit comfortably and close your eyes. Inhale and exhale ten times, slowly and deeply.
2. Focus your attention on the location of the third eye chakra, imagine a violet sphere of energy in the middle of your forehead. Remember, purple is the third eye chakra's color.
3. As you continue to breathe slowly and deeply, picture the purple ball of energy getting bigger and warmer. As it does, imagine it purging negativity from your body.
4. Think of yourself of absorbing the third eye chakra's energy—allow yourself to feel it all over.
5. Open your eyes when you feel ready.

Day 18 Third Eye Chakra Spiritual Meditation

1. Sit comfortably in a meditation posture which is comfortable for you. This can be on a yoga mat, cushion or a chair.
2. Close your eyes and take in three normal breaths, focusing on the flow of the air throughout your body.
3. Envision a white colored disk of energy rotating slowly at the top of your head.
4. Imagine a violet ray of light reaching up to the sky.
5. Then envision an additional violet beam coming from the sky to your white disk.
6. Allow this violet beam to flow downwards through each chakra down to the muladhara and into the earth.
7. Concentrate upon the light and let it envelop your entire body.
8. Chant "Shaam" as you are exhaling.
9. Meditate on this energy for 20 minutes.
10. When you are done, slowly open your eyes and take your time getting back to your feet.

Chapter 10 - Crown Chakra Reiki Meditation Day Nineteen Through Twenty-one

Overview of the Sahasrara Chakra - Crown or 7th Chakra

The crown chakra is located at the very top of the head and encompasses the elements of all of the chakras. It is associated with spirituality, communication with the Divine, union, ideas, awareness, thought, consciousness and nothingness which includes everything. The part of the body which are affected by the 7th chakra are the nervous system, brain and head.

Since the sahasrara chakra is where Kundalini Shakti reunites with infinite wisdom, it is the last element in completing your Kundalini awakening. When the prana and Kundalini flow through to your 7th chakra, there is a blossoming of your consciousness. The color of this chakra is violet and leads to love-infused prana. As this energy is flowing, the pineal gland is further activated which leads to a vibrating feeling at the top of the head.

When this chakra is open, clear and balanced, Kundalini Shakti is able to freely flow and you will be connected to the divine source within you. It is the final step of the process. However, you will need to continue to work on keeping your chakras clear and charged to allow this prana to continuously flow. However, for this state of being, it is rather difficult to keep up with daily tasks in the West as we know it.

Responsibilities of the Crown Chakra

The 7th chakra is located at the top of your head, which is why it is known also as the crown chakra. It is your source of spiritual connectivity and has an influence on the following:

- ❖ Self-worth
- ❖ Capability of finding peace
- ❖ Restful sleep
- ❖ Motivation to reach goals
- ❖ Excitement levels
- ❖ The level of beauty you see in the world around you.

Imbalance Symptoms

When your crown chakra is in alignment, you will experience a high level of pleasure in life. You will experience joy and gratitude along with spiritual awareness. When your 7th chakra is out of balance, you will likely experience issues with restless, melancholy, boredom and disillusionment. Other symptoms of an overactive crown chakra are the following:

- ❖ Self-destructive habits
- ❖ Disconnect from your spirituality
- ❖ Apathy
- ❖ Cynicism
- ❖ Desire to oversleep
- ❖ Lack of inspiration
- ❖ Confusion on which direction you should take in life
- ❖ Exhaustion
- ❖ Chronic tension headaches
- ❖ Poor coordination
- ❖ Depression

There are several reasons why your crown chakra can become blocked. Some common ways are coined as mid-life crises when you are reevaluating components of your life such as your relationship or career. Other ways are conflict in family relationships and negative feedback on projects that you are proud of.

Because this is the top chakra, it incorporates all of the aforementioned elements of earth, water, fire, air, ether and light. To balance out the energy of the crown chakra, spend quiet time in prayer, chanting mantras and meditation. There are no necessary changes needed for the diet.

Day 19 Crown Chakra Physical Meditation

1. Sit in a comfortable position where you will not be disturbed. Keep your back straight and your legs uncrossed. Place your hands on your your upper legs with your palms facing upwards.
2. Close your eyes and breath in through your nose and out through your mouth in three long and deep breaths.
3. Ponder upon a problem or personal blockage that needs attention. Visualize this problem in your mind.

4. Start chanting "Om" as you exhale. Become one with the energy that you start to feel.

5. Envision a white ball of flame in the heart chakra. With each breath, see this light get brighter and larger to envelop your entire body.

6. Continue to focus on the breath as this white flame spreads at a minimum of three feet from your body on all sides.

7. Now visualize a small violet colored flame by starting in the same fashion as you created the white flame. You will cover this white flame with the violet flame when you are complete.

8. Repeat the intention "I AM the Violet Flame of presence, blazing and transforming whatever within me that needs to be healed." Repeat this intention as many time as you need.

9. Feel the sensation of the energy throughout your being and continue to focus on your breath.

10. When you have finished, slowly open your eyes and stand slowly back on your feet.

Day 20 Crown Chakra Mental Meditation

1. Get comfortable while sitting in a chair with your back straight and your feet on the floor.
2. Put your hands in your lap overlapping each other and turn your palms to the sky.
3. Close your eyes and inhale through your nose and exhaling through your mouth.
4. Envision a lotus flower at the top of your head.
5. Continue to breathe slowly and evenly and see the lotus petals unfurling. There is a vibrant violet light in the middle of the lotus.
6. Focus on your breathing as you see the light getting brighter and more vibrant.
7. Feel the sensation of warmth at the crown of your head.
8. Allow the warmth to flow downwards throughout your whole body.
9. Sit with the sensations of warmth and continue to focus on your breath for ten minutes.
10. Slowly open your eyes and sit quietly for a few minutes before you get back up on your feet.

Day 21 Crown Chakra Spiritual Meditation

1. Sit comfortably in a meditation posture which is comfortable for you. This can be on a yoga mat, cushion or a chair.

2. Close your eyes and take in three normal breaths, focusing on the flow of the air throughout your body.

3. Bring your hands up to your face and cover your closed eyelids with the middle and ring fingers.

4. Place your index finger on your eyebrows and your pinky fingers on your cheekbones.

5. Breathe in deeply through the nose. As you exhale, chant "Om" with the "m" being drawn out, creating a buzzing sound.

6. Continue meditating and chanting for five minutes.

7. When the exercise is complete, slowly lower your hands and open your eyes. Take your time moving when you are comfortable to do so.

Chapter 11 - Daily Practical Tips

It can seem like a daunting task at times when you get into a negative cycle of thinking to snap yourself out of it. Many times empaths feel like they need to rant to express the pent up collection of emotions that they are feeling. Sometimes there just does not seem like any other way to feel balanced and sane again. However, this is not always the best approach.

Ideally, you will try to keep negativity out of your life altogether as you realize that it does not serve you and only brings your mind and energy down to a low level. How are you able to be the best you can be when you are feeling miserable? Of course you can use the self-care tools which are in chapter 4. However, there are further measures you can take to ensure that negativity does not cloud your energy and ultimately your day.

Center Yourself in Love and Truth

When you are not centered in your energy, this gives the person that you are interacting with the perfect opportunity to take advantage of syphoning your energy from you. The ego in the other person is driven to be fed and will drain you of your energy at any given moment as the ego is very selfish.

Signs that you are not centered are you will start to react to things that happen either in a conversation with another or a scenario that has happened in your environment. When you realize that you are reacting, especially out of emotion, you need to take a moment to recenter your energy.

Deep breathing exercises and meditations will help you to continue to stay in your calm, loving and true center. When you start to practice these daily, you will notice that you will not be as reactive with people or situations, and you will not become as drained and drawn to the negativity.

When you practice these centering activities, you are noticing your actions and thoughts from an impartial standpoint. It is as if you are seeing yourself from outside of your body. You are in a higher place and can see things for what they are. When you are in this state, you have achieved a balance based in love and truth. The longer you stay in this space, the deeper the connection will be with your inner voice and intuition.

Do Not See the World in Black and White

When you try to figure out what is "right" and "wrong" you are fighting a losing battle. The ego comes in to play and makes you think that everything that you are doing everything right, even if your gut tells you otherwise. When you just accept things as they are and not try to figure out what is right from an intellectual standpoint, you will be able to listen to what your intuition is trying to tell you to do.

This also means that you should not try to figure out the reasoning for negativity in another person's ego. When you start down this path, it will only start to feed your ego or their ego will start to drain your energy. Instead, continue to focus on your true purpose and determine if this person needs to be spending any more time with you.

If their ego is starting to go in a negative way by extending guilt, shame, blame or even start attacking you and your purpose, simply take note. Do not engage or react. This is exactly what the other person's ego wants as it will take the opportunity to take more energy from you.

Save Your Energy

When you are navigating through another person's emotions while you are not centered, you will certainly start to feel depleted of your energy. When you start to feel your energy start to dip, fill yourself up with light in every way possible. This should be done on an emotional, mental and physical way. Not only will it protect your energy from continuing to be drained, it will lift your spirits higher. Soon, your energy will be one that does not resonate with the energy vampire, and they will likely leave.

When you are able to save your energy from people who are trying to take advantage of you, this leaves you available for the people who need your help and will appreciate it. They will not willing take your light and energy away; they will welcome it. You will also see the benefit in helping and talking with people who are only wanting to lift each other up higher.

You Come First

Allowing yourself to come first is quiet effective when utilized on a regular basis. When you make sure that you practice your self-care each day and you ensure that your needs are met each day, this will prioritize your energy to where it needs to flow.

Remember, you are only able to be an effective psychic when your energy is centered and balanced. When you do not put your needs first, your time and energy will likely be spent on other people's needs. You will not be able to find the balance that you need while experiencing the world as a psychic or sensitive person in this way.

Effective Practices to Protect Yourself from Negativity

When you have negative energy attached to your body, there are several signs to warn you which are:

- Negative thinking
- Mood swings and emotions being uncontrollable
- Uncharacteristic impulsiveness

- Headaches and stomachaches that will not go away
- Inability to sleep
- Feeling of restlessness
- Feeling of depression, anxiousness or simply down
- Suddenly feeling drained or tired
- Not feeling like doing your regular routine

No matter where we go, there is negative energy which can infiltrate our energy levels and bodies. They can come from people or environments and it makes you feel more negative even when there is no immediate cause. When the dense energy affects your energy levels, you may feel a dip in your alertness and productivity. When it is found in your body, you will start to have physical symptoms such as headaches or pains throughout the body which cannot be readily explained.

Luckily, there are many different methods that can be used singularly or in combination to help you to rid yourself of the negative energies and get you back into a good place.

Herbal Smudging Stick - You can utilize an herbal smudging stick which can be used on yourself and your immediate environment. They usually come small hand tied bundles of Sweetgrass, Cedar, Mugwart, Rosemary or the most popular White Sage. They can also be in the form of incense sticks as they are a more concentrated form of the herbal bundles.

Light the top of the herbal bundle or incense stick and move it in a circular motion so that the fire is put out and it is just smoking. Continue to circle around the body by motioning around each of your seven main chakras and then around your whole body. The power of intention is necessary to clear out any negative thoughts or energies. Just thinking about the dense energy leaving your body will free its grasp on you.

If you want to smudge your house, simply walk around each room and permeate the rooms with the smoke. Pay special attention to where stagnant energy will rest underneath furniture and in corners. It is helpful to open the windows so that it invites the negative energies to vacate the house. Again, visualize these energies dissipating from your space while you are performing the smudging.

Saying a Mantra or Protection Prayer - As there are many choices as to what prayers or mantras to say, choose one that resonates with you and stick with it during the times you are clearing your energy. When you switch back and forth between different mantras during a clearing session, it confuses the energy.

Recite this mantra with emphasis and belief. When you think that it might work, it will not gain the power that it requires to work. You must absolutely believe these prayers are going to work with no doubt in your mind. This is when they are able to do their most powerful work.

Before you start to say the mantra, ask for your higher power to protect and aid you in ridding your body and environment from this negative energy. Ask for the energy to leave your body and remind that it does not have any power over you. Then start to take deep and deliberate cleansing breaths while visualizing a bright white light in a bubble around your body.

Start to say the prayer or mantra while visualizing the negative energy leaving your body and space. Say this prayer until you feel a general peace about you. Continue to keep the white light around you during and after the session to continue to strengthen your energy field to protect against the negative energies coming back into your body.

Dissipate the Energy with Noise - Everything in the Universe is comprised of vibrations. Some are denser than others, but this also means that it can be affected by other vibrations. When the energy in the environment seems too dense, make noise with your hands or start drumming if able to dissipate this energy. It will introduce a new vibration and will force the denser energy to break apart. You can simply clap your hands three times or you can incorporate this clapping exercise into a dance if you choose to continue to raise your spirits.

Physically Remove the Negative Energy - Use your hands to physically take the energy out and off of your body. This is something that can easily be done anywhere and will work quickly to help rid yourself of the negativity. Simply place your hands with your fingers together and move your hand across your body in a diagonal fashion.

While you are doing this, visualize dusting this energy off of your body.

Use Protective Visualization - In the middle of your chest, picture a ball of golden light while you are taking deep breaths in and out. While you are breathing, imagine this ball of light growing larger with each breath you take in. Expand this golden light until it covers your entire body and then approximately three feet away from the body on all sides to protect your aura.

Take a Bath or Shower - You can soak in a bath to release these dense energies from your body. Use a combination of 1 cup of baking soda with 1 cup of sea salt. You can mix this combination into a full bath or utilize this remedy while performing a foot bath by cutting the recipe into a quarter. Both will be effective in making your feel calmer, grounded and cleansed. If you are taking a shower, you can bundle some lavender or rose at the shower head to create a sweet and calming effect.

The Power of Thought - What you think becomes your life. When you focus and stress about all the things that are not making you happy in life, then you will only bring more stressful events into your life. Instead, shift your thinking to be more grateful for the things that you do have which make your life that much easier. Even look at the simple things as they will compound much easier. When you shift your thinking, you will automatically clear the negative energy in your body and around you as these two types of energy cannot coexist.

Remove the Negative People - When you find that you are constantly feeling drained about a certain person or group, you need to think about the positive benefits these people are bringing to your life compared to the negative effects. Usually the good will not outweigh the bad in these instances when the negative effect is very great. Instead, find more positive and happy people to spend your time with as you become like the four people you are closest to your life.

Take A Walk - Dense energies literally drain away your energy and make you want to stay stagnant. When you become active, the negative energy will have less of a hold on you. It can be as simple as going for a short walk to help clear your head or going on a day trip to your favorite place to spend some me time.

Mindful Meditation - When you are feeling stressed out or pulled in too many directions, find a quiet place to sit and start breathing in several deep and intentional breaths. With each inhalation, imagine you are taking in the power of your higher source and then breathing out the negativity you want to rid yourself of. When you are feeling more grounded, start to clear your mind of all random thoughts until you find peace. This may take a few minutes or an hour, but it will calm your energy as well as clear the negativity away.

Just Let it Go - When you hold grudges or negative ideas about places and people, it takes a toll on your body. These emotions will attach onto you if you allow them to. However, if you simply let these emotions go when they appear, they will not have this hold on your and not infiltrate your energy field. Acknowledge how you are feeling but do not internalize the emotions. Simply breath and visualize these emotions floating away if they do get attached.

Get Moving - This can include any type of exercise to include running or even dancing. Moving your body helps to invigorate the organs in the body as the blood starts to flow. Stagnant energy cannot be present when you are on the move which will keep negative energy from clutching onto you. Also, you are getting a little healthier each time you get out while doing something that you enjoy.

Music Cures Everything - Put on your favorite tunes which help to lift your spirit. Try to refrain from any depressing music. Feel the pulsing go through your body as it energizes your system and start to feel more upbeat. Find some new music who are similar to other artists that you enjoy to broaden your music collection and find songs that have positive lyrics and messages.

Sincere Gratitude - Just as positivity and negativity cannot exist in the same space, if you practice gratitude for what you have in your life, this will dissipate negative thoughts and energy. Consider writing down the people and events that you are thankful for. If you are having difficulty coming up with things to write, ponder about how there are many people in the world who are much worse off than you. When you understand that everyone in life goes through ups and downs, it helps you realize the bigger picture.

Inner Child Nurturing - Act and play with your inner child by putting your favorite happy song on the stereo system and sing at the top of your lungs. Even better if you dance along as if no one is watching. When you let yourself go in this positive way, the negative energy will lift very quickly. If singing is not your thing, find some silly jokes online or a favorite funny video.

Let Nature Shine - If your house or office is feeling negative and stagnant, open the windows or doors and let the breeze bring some new air and energy into the space. The sunshine will also couple well with the new air and you will feel revitalized, keeping negativity at bay.

Conclusion

I hope you enjoyed your copy of *Chakra Meditation: 21 Days Guided Meditation to Awaken your Spiritual Power, Reduce Stress & Anxiety and Improve Awareness of Psychic Abilities with Reiki Healing Exercises.* Let us hope it gave you all of the information that you were searching for about how to use Reiki and meditation techniques to heal yourself as well what you needed to get started in delving into the psychic abilities that we all posses.

The next step is to start working on the exercises which are going to strengthen your intuitive and psychic skills which will continue to compound into enjoyed benefits. There is no reason to be discouraged about your particular talents. When you continue to work with embracing and appreciating yourself for being a unique human being, the more confident and comfortable in your skin you will become.

When you are starting to apply the knowledge in this book, it is best to write down what your particular goals are so that you will have direction and not be side tracked. When you start to work with each goal individually, you will come to master your skills and goals at a higher rate. It will also help to keep you motivated towards the reasons you started in the first place.

Remember to keep your energies and thoughts balanced so that you do not feel overwhelmed. Utilize the methods in having more control over what emotions and sensations that you experience so that you are able to continue to fortify your skills. When you use this book to have more understanding about yourself, you will become your greatest self which will be able to help others much deeper than what you are capable of now.

Once you make it through the initial 21 days of the reiki meditation, be sure to keep it going. Take note where you body is still having issues, and work with the corresponding chakra. Keeping your energy clear and clean is an ongoing process, but you will know where and what to do now when a problem arrises.

When you finally start to embrace yourself for the beautiful soul that you are, you will start to realize all the benefits and gifts that come with living your life truly connected. Other than growing into a strong, deeper and connected individual, you will make a large impact in your family, community and even the world with your talents. The sky is the limit, and only you are limiting yourself in this matter.

I wish you luck while you continue down your paths in your journey. Remember to always trust your intuition as it will never steer you wrong, and have faith that you will be able to master all aspects of your psychic abilities so that you will shine at your brightest at all times. Also keep up with the meditation practices as they will continue to benefit you for some time to come.

Finally, if you found this book useful in any way, a review on Amazon is always appreciated! Thank you!

Lightning Source UK Ltd.
Milton Keynes UK
UKHW021426281120
374218UK00011B/730